T0022334

UNCOPYABLE SALES SECRETS

UNCOPYABLE SALES SECRETS

HOW TO CREATE AN UNFAIR ADVANTAGE AND OUTSELL YOUR COMPETITION

MAKE MORE SALES,
GROW YOUR NETWORK,
AND BECOME A TOP EARNER!

KAY MILLER

© Copyright 2022–Kay Miller

All rights reserved. This book is protected by the copyright laws of the United States of America. No part of this publication may be reproduced, stored in or introduced into a retrieval system, or transmitted, in any form or by any means (electronic, mechanical, photocopying, recording or otherwise), without the prior written permission of the publisher. For permissions requests, contact the publisher, addressed "Attention: Permissions Coordinator," at the address below.

Published and distributed by:
SOUND WISDOM
P.O. Box 310
Shippensburg, PA 17257-0310
717-530-2122

info@soundwisdom.com

www.soundwisdom.com

While efforts have been made to verify information contained in this publication, neither the author nor the publisher assumes any responsibility for errors, inaccuracies, or omissions. While this publication is chock-full of useful, practical information; it is not intended to be legal or accounting advice. All readers are advised to seek competent lawyers and accountants to follow laws and regulations that may apply to specific situations. The reader of this publication assumes responsibility for the use of the information. The author and publisher assume no responsibility or liability whatsoever on the behalf of the reader of this publication.

The scanning, uploading and distribution of this publication via the Internet or via any other means without the permission of the publisher is illegal and punishable by law. Please purchase only authorized editions and do not participate in or encourage piracy of copyrightable materials.

ISBN 13 TP: 978-1-64095-363-5

ISBN 13 eBook: 978-1-64095-364-2

For Worldwide Distribution, Printed in the U.S.A.

1 2 3 4 5 6 7 8 / 26 25 24 23 22

To Steve – my best friend, my partner in
business and life. You're still the one!

To Kelly – my daughter, the light of my life,
and my inspiration. I'll love you forever.

To YOU – the reader who is committed to being
an Uncopyable salesperson. You've got this!

CONTENTS

INTRODUCTION

Full disclosure: my first sales call was a disaster.

It was shortly after I started my outside sales career, just after college. I'd been passed over by several companies during the on-campus college recruiting process before being hired by Amerock, an industry leader in decorative and functional cabinet hardware. I was the first woman they'd ever hired for outside sales, which at the time was a very big deal.

During the interview, I was told that Amerock wanted to add women to their workforce, but they were nervous about how it would work out. I was grilled by the head of HR: "Ninety-nine percent of your prospects and customers will be men. We need to be sure that won't intimidate you."

I assured him it wouldn't. He wasn't convinced. "You'll be calling on construction, hardware, and lumber businesses," he continued. "How is that gonna work for you?"

I leaned forward and looked him in the eye. "I won't be intimidated," I said. "I can absolutely do this. I'll make calls, sell the product, and grow this territory. You'll be glad you hired me."

Fast-forward to my first solo prospecting call. I'd gone through the sales training at company headquarters in Rockford, Illinois. I'd compiled a list of prospects. I'd strategized my approach. My first call would be on a lumberyard called Blackstock Lumber, near my apartment in Seattle. I figured most sales reps would call for an appointment. Or they'd make a cold call and try to make a sale. My goal would be to stop by, meet the manager, and "build rapport," like I'd been taught. Only then would I ask to schedule a sales call.

I'd driven by and studied the layout: There was a big parking lot next to the road. The lumberyard was on the right, the retail store and office on the left. I was nervous but excited. Here was my chance to live up to that "you'll be glad you hired me" promise. I loaded freshly printed business cards into the briefcase my parents gave me when I got the job. I wore a professional outfit, right down to the bow tie I'd pinned to the neck of my button-down shirt. I slipped behind the wheel of my brand-new company car—a silver Buick Skylark (I called it my "grandpa-mobile." I didn't care; it was a big upgrade from the beater I'd driven throughout college. Even better, it was FREE!).

I drove the familiar route and pulled into the parking lot at Blackstock Lumber. That's when things fell apart.

A huge load of lumber had obviously just been delivered. There weren't any other cars in the parking lot, only trucks. Men in Levi's, flannel shirts, and hard hats swarmed around the lumberyard in frenetic activity. Forklifts plucked boards of various shapes and sizes from flatbed trucks, then hoisted them high above, secured with giant straps. The beams swayed back and forth as they were transferred to their various destinations.

I eased into a parking spot between two large work trucks.

There I was, a 24-year-old sales newbie. I suddenly realized I stood out like a sore thumb. It felt like everyone stopped what they were doing and stared at me. I'd been shy growing up, and those uncomfortable feelings came flooding back as I sat in the parking lot at the crowded lumberyard. I felt my face turn red. My palms were suddenly damp on the steering wheel.

I gave myself a pep talk. *This is what you signed up for*, I told myself. *You said you wouldn't be intimidated. You said you could do this, and you CAN.*

I sat there, peering through the windshields of the neighboring trucks at the entrance of the retail store. *All you have to do is walk across the parking lot. Open the front door. Go in like you know what you're doing.*

But I didn't. I watched myself peel a sweaty hand off the steering wheel, as if it was an out-of-body experience. I shifted the car into reverse. Then I sheepishly backed out.

Expletive! My face was on fire. I hit the accelerator and drove toward the exit as fast as I could. I felt all those eyes boring holes in the back of my head.

As I sped down the road away from my first prospect, I was *furious* with myself. I cursed myself for chickening out on my very first sales call.

Why am I telling you this? Because as salespeople, we all have failures. That day at the lumberyard, I failed about as much as a salesperson could.

After building a successful sales career, I can look back on this experience and recognize how my fear was distorting reality. The lumberyard seemed bigger than it was. Everyone was so busy; they probably weren't staring at me.

I was determined to go back, even if I risked looking like a fool.

The next morning, I steered my shiny Buick Skylark toward Blackstock Lumber once again. Just like before, I was dressed professionally and carrying my briefcase. I pulled into a parking spot. This time, I was determined not to slink away in fear. I took a deep breath and got out of the car. Yes, my heart was beating faster than normal, but I walked through the parking lot, past the busy lumberyard, and to the entrance. I looked straight ahead. If people were staring, I didn't care.

I made it to the door and went inside. I asked for the manager and introduced myself. We made small talk for a few minutes. Then, I asked if he'd be willing to schedule an appointment so I could learn more about him and his business.

Two months later, Blackstock Lumber had a small display of Amerock products in their decorative cabinet hardware section. The owner and I developed a good relationship, and eventually they upgraded to a much larger selection.

Fast-forward seven years. After being successful with Amerock, I'd changed companies—I was now a territory manager for Walker, one of the world's largest manufacturers of automotive exhaust systems. (I sold mufflers!) It was the final night of the National Sales Meeting and time for the Annual Sales Awards.

I knew my sales numbers were good based on the printout I got each week in the mail. I'd also received great feedback from my district manager. But I didn't expect what happened next. My name was called. I walked to the stage to the sound of thunderous applause. (Actually, I don't know if there was applause because I was in shock. But I'd like to think there was applause and that it was thunderous.)

The VP of sales handed me a large gold trophy—the first trophy I'd ever received! My name was engraved on the front. He congratulated me, announcing that I'd earned the award for achieving the highest sales in the nation. I was officially named Territory Manager of the Year. (Unofficially, I earned the nickname "Muffler Mama." What a claim to fame!)

How did I get from failure to success? What did I learn that allowed me to beat my competition and enjoy a successful sales career for all those years?

I learned to be an Uncopyable salesperson. Along the way, I developed a foolproof system I want to share with you. Here are the steps in the Uncopyable sales process:

Commit to a Win-Win Attitude

The Uncopyable sales process isn't adversarial. Tactics that are manipulative and pushy don't work anymore. Customers are a lot smarter these days—they want to be in control of the buying decision. As an Uncopyable salesperson with a win-win attitude, you provide a service to your customer. You guide them through the process that results in the very best decision for *them.* Making a sale that results in a happy, even excited customer is not just a win for the customer; it's a win for you, too. It leads to repeated sales, referrals, and testimonials. It's more profitable, and it's more fun.

Kick Fear's Ass

You won't make every sale. Even as an Uncopyable salesperson, failure is part of the process. You won't get through to every prospect, and you won't make every sale. There are times you'll be ignored, hung up on, and told "no"—or even "Go away!" When you overcome the fear of rejection, the fear of failure, and other fears that hinder your competition, you have a huge advantage. As an Uncopyable salesperson, you make more sales because you're willing to put yourself in uncomfortable situations. You do that by kicking fear's ass!

Craft a Personal Brand

Your customer isn't just buying your product or service—they're buying YOU. Who are you? What makes you different? And what's your brand promise? You'll learn the exact steps to building your own Uncopyable brand and becoming the Uncopyable salesperson your customers WANT to buy from.

Define Your Moose

In the Uncopyable philosophy, we refer to your ideal target market as your "Moose" (further explained in chapter 4). You might think your product or service is for everybody. But by narrowing your focus to the potential customers who are most likely to buy, you'll be able to get to know them better and do a better job of guiding them to the meaningful outcome they're looking for. You'll also waste less time, be rejected less often (yay!), and make more sales.

Get in the Door

The No. 1 complaint I hear from salespeople is they can't get in the door. Getting in the door can mean different things. You might want a prospect to take your call, set an appointment, or agree to find out more about your product or service. To do that, you have to capture their attention in a unique way. While most salespeople use the same old tactics to break through "the noise," the Uncopyable salesperson uses unique and creative communication methods to stand out—and get in the door.

Develop a
Mutually Trusting Relationship

People buy from people they know, like, and above all—trust. Follow specific strategies to build a solid relationship from your very first contact. Your ultimate goal is for your customer to see you as a trusted advisor—someone who will guide them in their buying decision. There are some basic actions to get your customer to know, like, and trust you. They're not difficult. The good news for you is most salespeople don't do them! Developing a mutually trusting relationship with your customer will set you apart from your competition—and grow your sales.

Think Like Sherlock Holmes

Your customer cares about what you can do for THEM. They want to work with someone who dedicates the time to get to know them and, most of all, what really matters to them. Put your detective skills to work—think like Sherlock Holmes—and uncover the exact points that will make them want to buy.

Follow Up

We all know that most salespeople don't follow up. The Uncopyable salesperson not only stays in touch, but also uses repeated contact to deliver even more compelling reasons for their customers to buy.

Get the YES!

As a salesperson, you can't wait to make the sale. But your customer doesn't want to be sold—they want to make the decision to buy. When your customer is just as excited about buying as you are about selling, well, that's the brass ring. Achieve that, and you're truly an Uncopyable salesperson.

"Okay, Kay," you might be saying, "but where are the secrets?" Here's the thing about secrets. A "secret" is simply something we don't know yet. It can also be something we know but don't understand—or even something we used to know but forgot about! The secrets I share in this book work. I've used them successfully—not to "close" my customers, but to help more of them buy. In the process, many of those customers have become friends. Now *that's* what I call a win-win!

When it comes to sales, there may be nothing new under the sun—it's just a matter of hearing it in a new and different way. That's often what it takes to give you the "aha" moment you need. I hope you enjoy reading these stories and secrets. Most of all, I hope you make more sales by putting these Uncopyable secrets into action!

Let's dig in.

SECTION ONE

BEFORE CONTACT

CHAPTER 1

WHEN THEY WIN, YOU WIN

I was almost 12, and I desperately wanted a new bike. I was still riding the single-speed Raleigh I'd gotten when I was 8. "It's dorky," I told my dad. Complaining didn't work.

By the end of the summer, I had my new bike. Even better, I had bought it myself—with money I earned. In the process, I fell in love with sales.

It was a hot June afternoon. School had just let out for summer break. I sat on the front porch with Mike, the kid who lived next door. I wanted a new bike. He wanted a baseball glove. We both needed money.

We were too young for real jobs—even babysitting (the local parents were too smart to trust us with their kids). I had the allowance I got for doing chores. I could count on some birthday cash from relatives. Not enough.

Mike and I brainstormed. *We should sell something*! Not lemonade—we'd seen other kids' failed attempts to pitch lukewarm Country Time.

Candy, we decided. It didn't take a genius to know the neighborhood kids wanted candy. *All kids want candy.*

It hit us. We realized the younger kids had a problem: They couldn't go to the store on their own. Even if they had money, they were too little.

Their problem was our opportunity! We would sell a product they wanted. We'd provide a service they couldn't get—we'd bring the candy *to them*. We'd charge a premium for that extra service and make a tidy profit.

In those days, the bottom shelf of the candy section at our local 7-Eleven was lined with an assortment of "penny candy."

"Let's sell penny candy for two cents!" Mike said.

Even at double the price, we figured it was a good deal.

We each raced home to raid our piggy banks. Mike stuffed our "seed money" into his pocket, hopped on his bike, and sped down the hill toward 7-Eleven.

I got to work. I found a plywood scrap behind my dad's work bench, balanced it on dusty lawn furniture, and neatly wrote, "Kandy Korner" on the lid of an old shoe box. (I've always loved alliteration!)

Mike returned with a brown paper bag bulging with an assortment of Smarties, bubble gum, and even candy cigarettes (an actual candy they sold in the olden days). I lined everything up in neat rows. We were in business!

Word spread like wildfire. Soon there was a line of kids snaking through the yard. One by one, they'd walk up to the table, eyes wide with excitement. They'd make their selections, then walk away, leaving a trail of candy wrappers.

When we ran out of candy, Mike pocketed some of our profits and rode back to 7-Eleven to restock. We'd started the perfect business—the money was rolling in! Our customers were just as excited to buy the candy as we were to sell it. It was truly a win-win.

Everyone was happy, until…

We got complaints. Not from customers. The complaints came from those age-old spoilers of fun: the MOMS.

"Mrs. Russell called," my mom said. Her tone of voice tipped me off—there was trouble. "She's pretty ticked off about her kids eating all that candy. She gave me an earful."

Unfortunately, that was it. We were officially shut down. It was a blow, but by the end of the summer, when I added my half of the profits to my allowance and birthday card money, it was enough for my bike! My success, and my new bike, were achieved through making sales. My lifelong career was unofficially launched.

It's All about the Customer

You can't beat the satisfaction—not to mention the adrenaline rush—of making a sale that benefits both you and the customer. But according to a 2021 *Wall Street Journal* article, people have become reluctant to work in sales.[1] Why? Because they still think of selling the "old school" way: cold calls, manipulation, and high-pressure closing techniques. That kind of sales relationship never worked for me. Fortunately, things have changed. These days, salespeople who are the most successful focus on relationships, problem-solving, and maximizing customer value. This shift in culture has benefited both the seller and the buyer.

Have you ever been in a situation where a salesperson's goal is to "close" you? My husband, Steve, and I once sat through an Orlando timeshare presentation. Afterward, one of the salespeople led us to his desk for a private meeting. He was obviously a "closer." We were immediately put off by his hardcore sales pitch.

This guy did all the talking. He spouted the features of the timeshare without asking any questions. He didn't take time to find out what we were interested in, where we wanted to travel, or what kind of vacation experience we were looking for. What he *did* do was tell us why we couldn't pass on this deal. Of course, there was a catch: the offer was only good if we said "yes" ON THE SPOT. None of the "advantages" he listed appealed to us. Some of the selling points were actually negatives: "You'll spend a week with your family in Orlando every year!" (Orlando? My family? Every year??) In the end, we decided to run, not walk, away from the timeshare.

We've all had someone try to talk us into something we didn't want. Think of a time someone tried to "sell you." How did it make you feel?

On the other hand, think of a time when a salesperson helped you buy something you were really happy with. Most likely, they got to know you, found out what was most important to you, and helped you get what you wanted. You were in the driver's seat, and you said "yes" because you believed it was the best decision you could make. Afterward, you felt good about the purchase.

We Don't Want to Be "Sold," But We Love to Buy

I remember a funny story about my niece, Shawna. When Shawna was little, my mom babysat her every Wednesday. Once when Shawna was about three, my mom told Shawna to pick up her toys so they could go to the store. Shawna's response: "I don't like to be *telled.*"

Shawna's three-year-old grammar made us laugh—but we agreed she had a point! None of us like to be "telled." We also don't like to be "selled."

A few years ago, Steve and I bought a new kitchen range (stove and oven combination). Some people spend a lot of time researching a purchase like that. Not us. We went straight to Sears (remember them?).

The salesperson, Gary, greeted us and asked what we were looking for. Steve pointed at me and said, "She's the decision-maker." Gary started with, "Tell me what you're looking for." He asked what I did and didn't like about my current range. He continued to ask more questions, which got me thinking about things I hadn't considered. "Do you normally cook for just the two of you, or do you like to entertain? Would it be helpful to save time on cooking? How about cleaning up?"

I told him I'd love a gas stove, but we weren't plumbed for it. He said, "It sounds like it's important that the burners heat up quickly."

After I answered all his questions, he responded with, "Let me show you the range I have." He led us over to the one he owned. (That's what he said, and I believed him.) It was electric, but he assured us, "You'll love how quickly the burners heat up." He added, "It has a convection oven. It doesn't need preheating, and it cooks more quickly than the one you have. You'll spend less time in the kitchen, and the kitchen will stay cooler during the hot summer months. (I'd mentioned that I don't like to use the oven in the summer for that reason.) In the end, Gary added a personal touch. "I'll throw in a bottle of this ceramic stove top cleaner. Just like you two, my wife cooks and I do the cleaning up. When I'm done, I use this special ceramic stove top cleaner, and I polish it until it shines." He added, "That can be Steve's job!"

"I'll take it!"

I didn't feel like I'd been sold...I felt like Gary had helped me make a great buying decision. That's a win-win.

As salespeople, we love to make sales. As customers, we want to buy. We want to make the decision. We want to feel like the product or service we choose is our idea. We want to work with salespeople who take the time to find out what's important to us and present their product or service in terms of what matters. Become a salesperson like that, and your customer will be as excited about buying as you are about making the sale. A sale like that leads to more sales—through repeat business, referrals, and testimonials.

When I started my first outside sales job with Amerock, I was tasked with selling more of our product to our largest distributor, Builders' Hardware & Supply (BHS). BHS was—and still is—a Seattle-area distributor. At the time I started, their purchases of Amerock decorative cabinet hardware had dropped. In fact, their purchases were at an all-time low.

I met the buyer, Jim Hentschell. Once I got to know him, he shared his Amerock sales numbers. I wanted to know where the Amerock line was selling the best and where it was lagging. He and I figured out Amerock's products were doing well with custom cabinet makers, who built and sold cabinetry for new construction and remodelers. On the other hand, their sales volume to the retail segment was disappointing.

I visited a few retail customers. These were mostly small, independent hardware stores—many were rural. As I visited the stores, I could see a lot of the retail displays were in terrible shape. Shelves were drooping, and products were covered with dust—or missing altogether. The best-sellers weren't even stocked.

As a distributor, BHS carried a wide assortment of product lines. The distributor salespeople called on a variety of accounts and were responsible for selling all their lines. Amerock retail displays weren't a big priority. But the neglected displays were hurting the distributor's sales—and mine. It was in both our interests to find a way to increase sales.

Jim and I pored over his sales reports. He thought their retailers had the wrong product assortment but wasn't sure how to fix it. I pointed out what I'd found at the stores—the displays were in bad shape.

"What if the displays were completely overhauled?" I asked. "What if they were revamped, restocked, and cleaned up? What if the best-sellers replaced the outdated duds?"

He agreed that would make a difference.

"I'll do it myself," I said.

I planned an epic road trip over the summer. I'd be visiting all BHS's customers in Washington State, including the eastern half of the state (it's not all green)! I packed my gold Samsonite suitcase, loaded up my trusty Buick Skylark, and off I went.

I went to each store carrying a red plastic caddy stocked with nuts and bolts, a cordless screwdriver, Windex, and some cleaning rags. Sometimes I sat on a borrowed stepladder. Sometimes I sat on the floor. I pulled products that weren't selling and carefully bagged and labeled them to take back to the warehouse for restocking. I repaired, straightened, and cleaned. I transformed each neglected display one by one into a neat and organized assortment of our top sellers.

It was a lot of work but also a lot of fun. I got to see small towns and parts of the state I never would have otherwise. A lot of these towns had funky tourist attractions and small historical museums. I stopped at them whenever I could. Some of them were surprisingly cool—like the Ohme Gardens in Wenatchee, Washington (if you're ever in the area, it's worth a visit!). It was fun to experience these slices of small-town life and meet the hardworking store owners and managers around the state. I enjoyed the people I met, and they appreciated what I was doing for them. When I called on those stores, I wasn't just stopping by to drop off catalogs and a business card. I was sincere about helping them be more successful. They appreciated this city girl who would come to their store in the morning and leave in the afternoon—hot, tired, and covered with dust. They'd often buy me lunch at their local cafés, and I never complained about the greasy hamburgers or see-through coffee.

Not long after I finished the project, I met with Jim. He beamed as he showed me the sales printout. "Our retail sales are up." They kept climbing.

A few months later, Jim asked me to meet him at his office once again. After we chatted for a bit, he reached into his desk and pulled out a piece of paper. "You've been talking about going to Europe," he said. It was true. It had been a dream of mine to take a trip to Europe with my friend, Teri.

The piece of paper turned out to be a check. "Your project significantly improved our retail sales. To show our appreciation, our company is buying your plane ticket. This check is from all of us!"

YOU CAN HAVE EVERYTHING IN LIFE YOU WANT, IF YOU WILL JUST HELP OTHER PEOPLE GET WHAT THEY WANT.

—ZIG ZIGLAR

My jaw dropped. I had helped BHS win big. And because of that, I won big.

To turn your customers into raving fans, look at what you're selling as a piece of the puzzle that makes up their world. Focus on them, not just what you're selling. When you do, you'll find opportunities to benefit customers beyond your product or service.

- What are their challenges, problems, and frustrations?

- What opportunities are they missing?

- What does the big picture look like to them?

Questions like these give you new ways to make a difference—to improve your customers' businesses and/or lives. That's the Uncopyable mindset, and it opens up the potential to create a true win-win.

Achieve that, and you'll build better customer relationships, create happier customers, and (here's the win for YOU!) make more sales.

BONUS CONTENT AND WORKBOOK AVAILABLE AT
UNCOPYABLESALES.COM/RESOURCES

CHAPTER 2

KICK FEAR'S ASS

Do you remember learning how to drive? Were you like me...
terrified? Did the other drivers make it even worse by honking and
"flipping the bird"? Did the whole experience make you want to go
home and hug your teddy bear?

For me, the scariest part was driving on the highway for the first
time. I clenched my teeth, accelerated, and merged my black '69 VW
Beetle into a line of cars resembling the Autobahn. I thought I was
about to die. My mom sat in the passenger seat, white-knuckled, pushing hard on an imaginary brake. Let's just say her body language wasn't
a confidence-builder!

I bet you can relate. You were afraid—but you pushed yourself past
that fear, didn't you? Maybe you stumbled and didn't pass the driver's test
the first time, but you went back, right? You've had your driver's license
for years now and don't give it a second thought.

The fact is, you've pushed past fear many times in your life. So what
is it about making that first sales call, or a cold call, so frightening...
even paralyzing?

Expand Your Comfort Zone

When I first called on Blackstock Lumber, I was way out of my comfort zone. I'd never made a cold call before. I don't even think I'd set foot in a lumberyard. Fear kept me from getting out of my car. I drove away, feeling like crap.

When I went back, walked across the parking lot and through the Blackstock front door, I proved to myself that I could do it. I went from the person who chickened out to the person who overcame fear, took a risk, and went inside.

What a great feeling.

Driving gets easier with experience. The same is true with sales calls. The more calls I made, the easier it got. Making cold calls that were the hardest gave me the most confidence. The best part about it? They were generally responsible for the most sales!

Being successful in sales requires risk. But we're not talking about life or death! When you force yourself to make calls other salespeople won't make, you separate yourself from the herd. Do what your competition is afraid to do. As a result, you'll make more sales, earn more money, and garner a lot of respect.

Unfortunately, there's no magic bullet. The only way to expand your comfort zone is to make yourself do the things you're afraid of. One sales manager I know urges his sales team to "get uncomfortable." Every time you push yourself to do something even though it makes you uncomfortable, you build confidence. Your self-esteem grows. Your brain literally creates new neural pathways.

If you want to nerd out, Google "neuroplasticity." Okay, I'll do it for you.

WINNERS MAKE
A HABIT OF DOING
THINGS LOSERS
DON'T DO!

According to VeryWellMind.com, neuroplasticity is defined as:

> *the brain's ability to change and adapt as a result of experience. When people say that the brain possesses plasticity, they are not suggesting that the brain is similar to plastic. Neuro refers to neurons, the nerve cells that are the building blocks of the brain and nervous system, and plasticity refers to the brain's malleability.*[2]

The article goes on to describe the two main types of neuroplasticity:

- *Functional plasticity: The brain's ability to move functions from a damaged area of the brain to other undamaged areas*

- *Structural plasticity: The brain's ability to actually change its physical structure as a result of learning*[3]

Obviously, I'm talking about structural plasticity here. The more you do something uncomfortable, the easier it gets. Your brain actually expands. Practice overcoming fear, and you'll strengthen your ability to conquer it, just like you'd build a muscle. Pretty soon momentum kicks in. You find that overcoming your fear makes it more fun!

Fear Is Good

If you don't ever feel nervous, you're not tackling the opportunities that will give you the biggest reward. The next time you're afraid to contact a prospect, ask for an order, or request a referral—and you do it anyway—pat yourself on the back. Acknowledge the feeling, because that means you're going for it.

A couple years ago, I found an organization that fit the profile of my "Moose"—my ideal buyer—perfectly. My goal was to book speeches with national organizations, and this one seemed like a perfect fit. The group was like others who had benefited the most from the Uncopyable philosophy.

I had used a *Get in the Door* strategy (I talk about that in chapter 5) and sent an autographed book directly to the CEO. When I followed up, I couldn't get through to him on his office line. I sent an email. He replied and said he'd forwarded my information to the Meetings Department. "They'll be in touch."

Great, I thought sarcastically. *I've fallen into a black hole called the Meetings Department. My name is on a long list. That doesn't make me stand out.*

I read through the CEO's email again. In the signature line, I saw his mobile number. *Hmmmm...*

I have nothing to lose, I thought as I dialed. Still, my heart was pounding. I almost hoped he wouldn't answer.

"Hello?"

I told him who I was and thanked him for taking my call. "Do you have a minute?" I asked.

"I don't," he answered abruptly. Then he continued, "If you call me back in a half hour, I can talk."

SCORE.

When I called back, I told him how a similar, but non-competing organization had benefited from the Uncopyable philosophy. I said I believed we might be able to provide the same value for his group. He agreed to set up a time to talk in more detail.

The committee would still be involved, but they now started out with a recommendation from their CEO. What a big difference from being "one in the pile"!

Those little wins are all stepping-stones on the sales journey, and I enjoy every one of them. Calls like that prove that to stand out, you need to be willing to take a risk.

Celebrate Failure

What if you ARE rejected or even thrown out? Congratulate yourself. It means you've left nothing on the table. Throughout my years in sales, I've been told NO. I've had people hang up on me. I've heard, "We don't want any!" I've been asked to leave—and not always nicely. As our friend Mark Victor Hansen says, "Next!"

You'll make way more sales if you take chances and are willing to miss. So, how do you do it? How do you make yourself do the very thing you're afraid to do? There's no way around it—the act of pushing through your discomfort is the very thing that makes you grow. Your reward? You'll make more sales!

It's essential that you force yourself to dive into uncomfortable situations. Here are some of the strategies that work for me.

I'VE MISSED MORE THAN 9,000 SHOTS IN MY CAREER. I'VE LOST ALMOST 300 GAMES. TWENTY-SIX TIMES I'VE BEEN TRUSTED TO TAKE THE GAME-WINNING SHOT AND MISSED. I'VE FAILED OVER AND OVER AND OVER AGAIN IN MY LIFE. AND THAT IS WHY I SUCCEED.
—MICHAEL JORDAN

Strategy 1: Ask Yourself Three Questions

1. What's the worst thing that can happen?

Unless it deals with driving a car in speeding traffic or a similarly dangerous behavior, you won't die. When I went back to Blackstock Lumber the second time, the worst possibilities were: being stared at, hearing the word "no," and maybe even getting thrown out. *I could survive those things*, I decided.

Convince yourself that you can handle the worst thing that could happen. *Because you can.*

2. How will I feel if I let fear stop me?

For me, the feeling of chickening out was worse than the risk of rejection. When you hold back, you're forced to define yourself as someone who lets fear stop them. That's not you.

3. How will I feel if I push past the fear?

There's nothing like overcoming a challenge to make you truly proud of yourself. Pushing past fear makes any accomplishment extra sweet. Doing something you're afraid of (in a good way) gives you confidence. It builds your self-esteem. You prove to yourself (and others) that you can do it. And best of all, you gain the momentum to achieve even more.

GOING BEYOND YOUR COMFORT ZONE DETERMINES THE SPEED AT WHICH YOU GROW.

Strategy 2: Positive Self-Talk and Affirmations

We all have a little voice in our heads. Unless you take control, that voice naturally defaults to the negative. (I'm pretty sure it's not just me.) Here are three ways to change that.

1. Internally

Have a mantra. My favorite—and the one I use for every challenge I take on—is simple: "I can do this." I repeat that line in my head every time I encounter a difficult experience. It helps me through fear, frustration, and uncertainty. In other words, it works!

Use affirmations. Write them down. Put them on Post-its, in your phone, or next to your bed. Here are some that might work for you:

- Customers WANT to buy from me.

- My product/service helps my customers.

- I'm confident.

- I'm pleasantly persistent.

Take the time now to write down—in your journal, on an index card, or even in the margins of this book—at least two other affirmations that will encourage you to persevere in the face of difficulty, regardless of how big or small the challenge.

2. Externally

Feed your brain. Read self-help books and biographies about people overcoming fears and challenges. Google "good news" for a whole bunch of stories on the Internet that will make you smile. Music is one of my favorite ways to get unstuck. I have a playlist called "Uplift," and every song on it pumps me up. Listening to music on my headphones can quickly put me in a whole new mindset. What music would you put on your "empowerment" playlist?

3. Visually

Create a visual. I have a bulletin board in my office that I've plastered with quotes and sayings, as well as pictures of various accomplishments and goals I'm working on. Here are three of the things on my board:

- A picture of me receiving my Territory Manager of the Year Award

- A picture of Einstein with the following quote: "A person who never made a mistake never tried anything new."

- A quotation from an anonymous source: "I like hard. Hard is where people give up. The more hard things I do, the less competition I have."

- A quotation from Gary Player: "The harder I work, the luckier I get."

Strategy 3: Be Like Superstars

Visualization

Have you ever watched a world-class athlete mentally prepare for competition?

I remember watching Lindsey Vonn on TV immediately before she was set to ski in a World Cup downhill race. The camera zoomed in close. Vonn's eyes were closed, head and arms moving smoothly side to side as she raced down the hill in her mind. She'd memorized the entire course and saw herself racing to victory before she launched through the gate. Did she win? Of course, she did—a total of 82 times over her amazing career.

When our daughter, Kelly, was a junior golfer, she went to an intensive golf camp called Vision 54. (Fifty-four is the score you'd shoot if you played every hole one under par—in other words, if you got a birdie on every hole.) As its title suggests, the program focused as much on the mental part of the game as the physical.

Athletes aren't the only superstars who visualize success. Dancers, musicians, surgeons, professional speakers, and yes, businesspeople use visualization techniques to enhance performance and achieve their dreams.

Like an athlete, you can create a clear mental picture of the result you want. Visualize the sales results you want. Then, visualize the steps you need to take to get there. Imagining is practice for the brain and makes the actual *doing* easier. Do your best to experience the feelings that will come when you achieve your goal. The more emotion you can conjure, the more powerful the visualization will be. Imagining the excitement and sense of accomplishment you'll feel when you reach your goal will help pull you through to that goal. Think about how you'll feel when you've earned that dream vacation for your family!

Write your story

Take some time to write exactly how you'd like your story to go. Start with the present. Write about what's happening now. Next, write the ideal progression you'd like to make. As you write the steps, practice the visualization technique described above. Imagine yourself taking the necessary steps, achieving the goal, and enjoying the results.

Meditation

Meditation has become a lot more mainstream lately. After giving it a half-hearted try for years, I've been giving it more effort. When Phil Mickelson won the 2021 PGA Golf Championship—becoming the oldest major tournament winner at age 50—he credited meditation with helping him focus. I thought, *I have to give this a serious try.*

Everyone has their own definition and application of meditation, but it usually involves an internal centering enabled by focusing on your breath. For me, meditation is the practice of letting go of the thoughts I don't want. Every time a thought invades my brain, I dismiss it and once again focus on my breath. This practice reinforces the habit of staying positive, which is critical to becoming an Uncopyable salesperson.

Strategy 4: Body Language

In her TED Talk that attracted over 60 million views, social psychologist Amy Cuddy made the case that "power posing"—standing in a posture of confidence, even when you don't feel particularly confident—can dramatically boost performance. In her studies, Cuddy discovered that using power poses helped people do better in mock interviews. They also had higher pain thresholds and reported feeling better about themselves overall.

Superheroes are well known for using power poses. My superhero of choice is Wonder Woman, since my husband, Steve, was once a stunt double for Lynda Carter on the TV show *Wonder Woman*. (She was tall. To keep the transition to the stunt double believable, they used men.)

Here are some effective "power poses":

- Strike a high-power pose such as standing erect like Wonder Woman, with your palms on your hips and your feet set at the distance of your shoulders, for two minutes.

- Imitate the "victory" move. (It's the "Y" you do on the dance floor when the DJ plays the song "YMCA"!) Winners of athletic events naturally strike this pose. I did it recently without thinking about it when I jumped into an ice-cold lake on a dare.

- Sit tall with your back straight, and breathe deeply.

If you're looking for one simple yet highly effective way to boost your confidence, try a power pose.

Your actions, thoughts, words, and body language all go into that supercomputer called your brain. Use them to your advantage.

Strategy 5: List Your Own Proof

You've done scary things before. Think about it—what have you done that made your palms sweat? I still remember the feeling of accomplishment when, at age 10, I finally jumped off the high dive. I was on top of the world!

What fears or challenges have you overcome? It could have been a physical feat or the time you gave a speech in front of the whole class. The person who did that was YOU. You overcame your fear. Use that proof to help you do it again.

Create new proof

A few years ago, I went zip-lining in Guatemala. One of my traveling companions, Marco, encouraged me to do it. Not only that—he challenged me to do it "Superman style." If I accepted the challenge, I'd "zip" down the mountain in a horizontal position, head first and face down. Just thinking about it made my palms sweat. But my competitive side kicked in. I said "yes."

As I was strapped into a bulky harness, high in the jungle near the city of Antigua, I asked myself, *What the hell am I doing?*

Still, I didn't back down. I closed my eyes and shouted "GO!" Honestly, I about pooped my pants when I shot off the tall platform and went sailing across the canyon. I was flying!

My comfort zone expanded at the same speed I flew down the mountain. When I landed, my No. 1 one thought was, *I did it!* That feeling of exhilaration was amazing.

As kids, we naturally want to try new things. We're anxious to show how brave we are. As adults, we still relish those accomplishments, but we need to push ourselves. The confidence we gain is worth it—and affects us on every level. By challenging yourself in non-sales situations, you build mental strength as a salesperson, too. An upbeat and confident attitude will help you find more prospective customers, persist with the prospects you have in your pipeline, and make you more persuasive. That translates to more sales!

Start a "kick fear's ass" journal

Every time you try something new or push past fear, write it down in your journal. Enjoy reliving the experience and celebrating your achievement. Pat yourself on the back!

A few years ago, our daughter, Kelly, had the opportunity to meet Jack Nicklaus. Kelly was a junior golfer at the time and happened to meet the famous golfer while practicing at her home course. Nicklaus was visiting the nearby golf course he'd designed—pro bono—specifically for veterans injured in combat, known as "Wounded Warriors." Kelly was thrilled. He was kind and approachable, and Kelly even got a picture with him. Later that night, Kelly told me and Steve the story and shared how much she admired him.

As one of the greatest players ever, Nicklaus is a role model for not only the physical game of golf, but also the mental side. Once, during an interview, Nicklaus was asked, "How can you stand on the 18th fairway of the U.S. Open knowing you HAVE to hit the next shot on the green to set up a victory? How do you manage the fear?"

YOU ARE IN A GREAT POSITION, RIGHT NOW, TO MOVE OUTSIDE OF YOUR COMFORT ZONE.

Nicklaus acknowledged that he'd been in that situation many times during his career. "I still get nervous," he said. "I get butterflies in my stomach—but I work hard to get them to fly in formation!"

Then he got serious. "Here's what I think of," Nicklaus said. "First of all, I remind myself that I am exactly where I WANT to be. I WANT to be in a position to win the U.S. Open. When I played by myself as a kid, I would always pretend I was standing on the 18th fairway needing to hit that next shot or needing to make a long putt to win a big tournament, like the U.S. Open. I WANT to be here."

Do you WANT to be a successful salesperson? Then the next time you get nervous before a prospecting call, meeting, or presentation, remind yourself that you're exactly where you WANT to be!

BONUS CONTENT AND WORKBOOK AVAILABLE AT

UNCOPYABLESALES.COM/RESOURCES

CHAPTER 3

CRAFT A PERSONAL BRAND

So, this is what it's like to install a muffler.

My arms strained under the weight of the welding torch above my head. Sparks showered over my Darth Vader-style helmet. A trickle of sweat ran down my back.

As a new territory manager with Walker, a leading manufacturer of automotive exhaust systems, I was accomplishing what I'd set out to do: learn about the product I was selling—automotive mufflers—*from the customer's perspective.*

Before I was hired by Walker, I didn't know much about cars, except how to drive one. (Even that is debatable—I once backed one of our family cars into the *other* one.)

I learned about my product line by:

a) going through the company training, and

b) studying product catalogs, brochures, and sales materials.

I could recite material thicknesses and statistics on the effects of back pressure on engine performance and fuel economy. But I had zero experience with the product and no idea what it was like to actually install a muffler.

I decided I needed to fix that. I went to Walt's Radiator and Muffler, one of my distributor's customers. I knew the manager, Wayne. "I'd like you to teach me how to install a muffler system," I told him.

I could tell he was skeptical. "Do you know how to weld?"

"Hmmm. I guess I need to learn that, too."

He looked down at the shoes I was wearing. Penny loafers. "Okay," he said in an amused tone. "But first, you'll need a pair of steel-toe boots."

I looked at his boots. How should I describe them? I guess the word would be...UGLY. They were clunky—mud brown with square toes to accommodate the fact that there was actual steel underneath. I remember thinking of the phrase "your mama wears combat boots."

He sensed my reluctance. "Unless you don't mind losing a toe," he added.

I definitely minded.

I made an appointment with Wayne for the following week. Later, I made my first trip ever to Red Wing Shoes. I tried on several pairs of steel-toe boots and chose the pair I felt were the least unattractive.

The next week, I found myself clomping across the parking lot of Walt's Radiator and Muffler. Wayne looked up—I'm sure he heard me coming (luckily, I was no longer afraid of being stared at)—and gave me what I considered to be a respectful nod.

I followed him out to the garage, where a car was perched high on a hydraulic lift. He motioned to the car's underbelly, where I saw our project: an old rusted-out muffler with holes in it.

Wayne handed me my gear. I took the set of heavy coveralls, thick gloves, and the aforementioned Darth Vader-style helmet. Wayne went to get the new muffler and hardware we'd need to install it. Meanwhile, a few mechanics milled around the shop, doing their best to seem nonchalant.

I watched while Wayne removed the old muffler. Next, he gave me a quick tutorial on using a (surprisingly heavy!) welding torch. Then I got to work. For the next 20 minutes, Wayne pointed here and there, giving me instructions as I attached the muffler and clamps, then welded everything to the exhaust pipes (he may have helped a little).

Before I go on, allow me to provide a little context. This happened in the late '80s. A few years earlier, a popular movie called *Flashdance* had been released. It's a feel-good movie starring Jennifer Beals, who faces obstacles in her quest to become a professional dancer.

In the opening scene of the movie, it's very dark. In the distance, you see sparks...and then flames. When the camera pans in, you realize the sparks and flames are coming from a person—a welder.

Suddenly, the flame goes dark. The sparks stop. The welding torch is laid down. The identity of the welder, who is covered from head to toe in welding armor, is still a mystery. Then, slowly, one arm reaches out and carefully lifts the welder's helmet. For the first time, you see the welder's face. I, along with everyone in the audience, assumed the welder was a man. But it's not. It's a *woman.* Not just any woman, either. As she lifts her helmet higher, you realize it's gorgeous, sexy Jennifer Beals.

Finally, her helmet is all the way off. She gives her head a toss. The dark curls of her hair cascade down her shoulders. The camera catches her perfect face, glistening with a light glow of perspiration.

This was the picture in my mind as I kept welding. *I'm just like Jennifer Beals in the opening of Flashdance!* It felt pretty cool. Eventually, we finished. The whole muffler system was installed perfectly.

I was ready for my Jennifer Beals moment. I put down my torch, just like Jennifer Beals. I lifted my helmet, just like Jennifer Beals. I gave my head a little toss…just like Jennifer Beals. But something didn't feel right.

As I stood there in all my Jennifer Beals-wannabe glory, I could tell the guys in the shop were watching.

I looked around at them with a smile that I'm sure was a little smug. Then I looked across the garage. Above the utility sink, there was a mirror.

I saw my reflection and stopped cold.

I looked like a sewer rat…a *wet* sewer rat.

I had no resemblance to Jennifer Beals. That "something that didn't feel right" was my hair. Instead of cascading down my shoulders like Jennifer's, my hair was plastered flat to my head with sweat. My face was red hot, mascara running down my cheeks.

I looked at Wayne, embarrassed. He smiled. "Same time tomorrow?"

Okay, so I didn't look like Jennifer Beals. But learning to weld did enable me to accomplish my goal: to prove my commitment to my customers. In my experience, when you care more, you sell more. This commitment to learning my customers' pain points so that I could help them make decisions that would improve their lives and businesses became my brand promise, the value I guaranteed every customer through our professional relationship.

Your Brand Promise—They're Buying YOU

You might not have realized you need a brand promise as a salesperson—after all, you're selling a product or service with its own brand promise! But in reality, as a salesperson, you're selling yourself as much, if not more, than your product or service. So, crafting a compelling brand promise is a critical part of perfecting your sales strategy. And the most effective brand promises have the customer at the heart of them.

No matter what kind of sales situation you're in, when your customer sees you as an asset, you become their ally. You're on their side and a key part of their success. As an Uncopyable salesperson, your personal brand is *your promise and what you represent to the customer.* You're not just part of what they're buying; *you're the most important part of the package.* Yes, they're buying the product or service, but they're also buying you and what you can do for them.

You want to be seen by the customers as unique and different. To do that, you need to set yourself apart. Take some time to think about what YOUR brand promise is. Don't get caught up in the thinking that you need the perfect product or service to beat the competition. (We've all heard stories of salespeople who switch organizations and take their customers with them.) It's important to realize true sales success isn't about the perfect product or service. It's how you build confidence in the solution you represent and work with the customer so they know you have their best interests at heart.

UNCOPYABLE SALES SECRETS

There's a lot of talk these days about how customers have gotten smarter and can no longer be manipulated, tricked, or talked into buying something they don't want. You and I are those customers! When you're a buyer, you're no dummy. Your customer isn't, either. People can tell when someone is genuinely interested in helping and when they're just trying to make a sale.

Having a brand promise makes selling more fun and more rewarding for both you and your customers. Plus, you make a lot more sales!

Brand Promise #1: Know and Believe in Your Solution

My welding story got around. People got a kick out of it—from customers to my fellow reps and management. Other people repeated it, and so did I. It became my signature story and symbolized part of my brand promise: *to know and believe in my solution.* The story proved how far I'd go to understand my product from the customer's perspective: I was willing to walk a mile in their shoes (errr...steel-toe boots)!

Brand Promise #2: Go the Extra Mile

Steve has a good friend and golf buddy named Kelly McCann. (My daughter's name also happens to be Kelly, and my husband's tagline is "Kelly's dad." In case you're wondering, YES, IT'S CONFUSING!)

Okay, just to clarify, this story is about Kelly the FRIEND and not Kelly our daughter!

THIS Kelly is a very successful salesperson for a Seattle distributor of industrial cleaning and janitorial products. He likes to say, "I sell toilet paper!" even though some of the products in his line cost thousands of dollars. Let's just say whatever he sells, he does it very well.

A few years ago, we had a big ice storm in Seattle. I mean, BIG. Our area sometimes gets a light dusting of snow in the winter. It's unusual to have more than that. But every once in a while, it dumps. This was one of those times. Schools closed (snow day!!). Many businesses even closed. Seattleites are snow wimps, for good reason. In Seattle, we have very few snowplows and fewer snow tires. What we do have: steep hills and slippery bridges.

During this particular snowstorm, Steve called Kelly. Steve had a sneaking suspicion that despite the snowstorm, Kelly was on the road. When Kelly answered his phone from his truck, Steve's suspicion was confirmed.

"What the heck are you doing out there?" he asked.

"I'm selling and delivering!!" Then Kelly added the now legendary line: "The toilet paper must go on!"

That was typical Kelly McCann.

Kelly has literally gotten up in the middle of the night to take care of customers. His success proves that a total commitment to the customer works. "I've heard from my competitors. Sometimes they call on one of my accounts. When they hear the words 'I work with Kelly McCann,' they know they don't stand a chance. They're basically just waiting for me to retire." (It's not bragging if it's true!) "I always keep an eye on my customers," he says, "and my phone's pretty much always on. I have relationships with the manufacturers, and if there are questions, I can get answers quicker than anybody. I keep track of rebates my customers have coming, so they know they're not missing out on anything. I tell every customer, 'Nobody will take care of you like I will.'"

To stand out from the competition, go the extra mile for your customer. A commitment to go above and beyond is a powerful secret to becoming an Uncopyable salesperson.

Brand Promise #3: Relationship over the Sale

I heard a great sales story recently from Dave Loomis of Loomis Marketing. Dave was impressed by a story a client told him and passed it on. His client has worked with a particular IT provider, he told me, ever since the client met a woman named Leslie:

> I brought them aboard in 2014. It was all Leslie. We'd been using [a competitor] and they turned into a Walmart. Then, I got a cold call out of the blue. Enter Leslie. I almost never take cold calls—but I did. She ended up giving me a presentation. I built a relationship. I didn't buy the company; I bought Leslie. She sold us on the concept of getting white glove treatment. The idea of somebody watching over us and keeping our best interests in mind was the kicker. I was tired of the bureaucratic "punch in and they spew out results" thing. It's about more than the cost. The cost is important, but I cannot afford the wrong product. My reputation is at stake. And that, as they say, is priceless.

Leslie's "white glove treatment" sets her apart. It's created such loyalty that her customers don't even mind paying a little more. When you're competing with others—including in your organization—have a brand promise that distinguishes you from everyone else.

Be Memorable

Memorable Color

It's pretty common to see organizations incorporate color into their branding, then produce stuff like coffee mugs, pens, water bottles, and T-shirts, all using that color, for giveaways. That's all well and good, but very common. Uncopyable salespeople don't do common things. I recommend taking it a step further: connect that color to you in every way possible.

My husband, Steve, and I are business partners. For years, we've helped organizations, business owners and salespeople significantly grow their businesses through speaking, consulting, books, and other educational products. Together, we've created the Uncopyable philosophy.

In a nutshell, the Uncopyable philosophy is based on completely separating your organization—and yourself—from the competition. Your goal isn't to be one possible choice but the ONLY choice. The central concept we teach is you shouldn't just look for ways to "get out of the box" but actually build your own box—creating your own rules of competition, establishing value that nobody else can or will be able to copy, and delivering a brand promise that people won't forget.

We walk our talk. For example, orange is the color we picked for our company, but it has become more than just a color that is loosely associated with our brand—we have connected it to every aspect of our business so that customers immediately think of the Uncopyable philosophy when they see it. We tell our clients that every time they see the color orange, they should be reminded to look for unique ideas and concepts that they can implement in their own business to make it Uncopyable. Naturally, they also think of us. We're so well known for the color orange that our clients and prospects even send us orange gifts!

I was on a Zoom call the other day with a new client. I say "new." Actually, it took five years for her to buy! When she finally decided to work with us, I found out we'd been on her mind the entire time—all because of the color orange. When she and I got on the Zoom call, she opened her top desk drawer and pulled out a CD in an orange case. Then she held up a pair of orange shoelaces. I'd sent both years before. "This is the 'How to Tie Your Shoelaces' video!" she told me.

She remembered us, and the Uncopyable brand, because of the color orange and the unconventional gift of shoelaces. I couldn't believe she still had them after all these years. I've made a surprising number of sales because people attach the color orange to us and to the idea of being Uncopyable. Owning a color—and going big—makes you memorable.

Memorable Word or Phrase

Take ownership of a word or a phrase, something that connects to your promise. A famous example is Volvo: When people are thinking about buying a new car, if their primary concern is "I've got to protect the kids," they're automatically going to think of Volvo, because Volvo owns the word "safety." It would be difficult to impossible for another company to steal that word from them. Another example: Disney World is known as "the happiest place on earth." Not "happy" or "happier"—"happiest." For Ben & Jerry's, the word is "quirky," and whatever they put out there has to reflect that quirkiness.

Several months after Steve's book *Uncopyable* was released, we got a call from Rhonda Wight, president of Refrigeration Sales Corporation, an HVAC and refrigeration wholesaler in Ohio and Pennsylvania. She told me how RSC was motivated to be Uncopyable and decided to choose a word that would reflect their commitment to customers. They got together as a team and chose the word "relentless."

On their website, here's how RSC defines their promise to the customer:

RELENTLESS: (adj) [ri-lent-lis]

Disciplined in Approach & Action, Never-Ceasing, Determined to Achieve, Be Sincere.

LIKE A DOG WITH A BONE, WE ARE RELENTLESS. ONCE WE START, WE WON'T STOP. WE CAN'T STOP! WE CARE AND WE DEMONSTRATE THAT WE CARE!

- *Ownership: We own the customer interaction, follow up and stay involved and proactively seek resolution.*

- *Sense of Urgency: We make meeting the customer expectation a priority, actively engage our fellow associates, and escalate issues when necessary.*

- *Passion: We care about what we are doing and we care about the customer that depends on us.*

We will let no customer problem go undetected or unre-solved. Each of us will take ownership for our actions and create customer responsiveness unequaled by our competi-tion. We believe that it is not the customer's responsibility to notify us of problems, but rather our responsibility to anticipate them. We will correct problem issues before they become an impediment to our customer's success.

They OWN the word "relentless." They embed it in all their mes-saging, anchoring it in their customers' minds. Nobody can steal that word from them.

This is just as applicable to salespeople. Remember Leslie and her promise of "white glove treatment"? She could own that phrase, using it as an anchor for selling to customers and helping them remember her. She could get pictures of herself with happy customers, both wearing white gloves. She could have a logo inspired by a white glove designed for herself.

Think about how, as a salesperson, you can own a word to help define who you are and what you want to represent. It's a secret you can use to separate yourself from the competition!

Memorable Business Card

If your business card is in a stack of others laid out on a table with ten of your competitors' cards, what makes it stand out? One of the Uncopyable mantras is "Look at what everyone else is doing, and don't do it." We all tend to look at our competition for ideas, but that makes you blend in with the crowd. If you have the flexibility to do it, design your own card. Make it really different. Steve and I both have orange business cards, and they both have cartoons designed on the back.

People notice and remember that. If our business cards end up in a stack with others, ours stand out!

Visit:

UNCOPYABLESALES.COM/RESOURCES

to see my business card and access additional bonus content to help you become an Uncopyable salesperson!

Memorable Title

Steve is "Kelly's Dad and Marketing Gunslinger." Tax analysts have branded themselves as "Tax Wranglers" and sales executives as "Sales Ninjas."[4] Being different might be uncomfortable, but if you want to succeed, set yourself apart with your own language. Remember, Kelly McCann says with pride, "I sell toilet paper!"

What does your title tell your prospect? If your card says the same thing as everyone else's—something like "Consultant for XYZ"—you don't stand out. Consider a title that's unique and memorable!

Materials

Again, if you hand out the same materials as everyone else, you blend in. It's easy to make custom materials in an online design program.

Make your materials personal, with your picture, and be different and memorable.

Language

Instead of using the phrase "target marketing," we call it "hunting Moose" (explained in chapter 4)—a concept we came up with. Our clients NEVER say "target market." They always talk about the Moose. It's ingrained in them, and when they use that language, it's immediately clear whom they learned it from. Of course, "Uncopyable" is also a word we coined. If you look up "Uncopyable," the only things that come up are Steve's book—and mine!

Something Quirky

I'm still known as Muffler Mama! Is there something quirky about you? (I sure hope so—quirky means interesting!) One of our clients, Jeff, is a ketchup fiend. He recently told me the story of the night he met his in-laws. They'd prepared steak and lobster for the newlyweds, and Jeff brought a bottle of ketchup! (Luckily, he and his wife had already eloped!) He also told me about his regular lunches at Ruth's Chris Steak House, where, in a previous position, he'd take customers out to lunch nearly every day. Of course, he asked for ketchup. At first, they said "no," but eventually, they compromised by bringing him a gravy boat of ketchup. It became part of his standing order.

Jeff pokes fun at himself for his ketchup addiction, and it's something everyone knows about. That gives him the opportunity to use his ketchup obsession to separate himself from the crowd. (Did you know you can find ketchup bottles on keychains? Talk about memorable!)

Anchor

One of our consulting projects was with Gallery Furniture in Houston, Texas. Gallery Furniture is a huge store (owner Jim McIngvale is well known for opening it up to Houston residents during recent weather events that have displaced them). Gallery Furniture has multiple salespeople walking the floor at any one time. When we worked with them, one of the salespeople shared something that was frustrating him. As the salesperson explained, he was good at greeting new customers when they walked through the door. He always offered to help. The problem was most people wanted to walk the huge showroom by themselves. By the time they were ready to talk to a salesperson, they grabbed the nearest one. He'd tried giving them his business card—the one that looked like everyone else's. They'd slip it in their purse or pocket and forget about it.

As we got to know the salesperson, we found out he always carried a lollipop in his hand. Our suggestion? Design a unique business card with a picture of him holding a lollipop. Print his cell phone number in BOLD. Then attach the card to a lollipop and give that small gift to shoppers when they come in. What a difference! The salesperson later reported that most customers would eat their lollipop while they were browsing. When they got to the point where they needed help, they called him on his cell phone!

Something that small can make a huge difference. Think about something you can do—small or large—that will make you stand out from everyone else—and be memorable!

BONUS CONTENT AND WORKBOOK AVAILABLE AT

UNCOPYABLESALES.COM/RESOURCES

CHAPTER 4

MOOSE STRATEGY

In Steve's best-selling book, *Uncopyable: How to Create an Unfair Advantage Over Your Competition* (yep, it's a mouthful), he uses "hunting Moose" as an analogy for finding your best prospects:

> *In 1986 I was a guest on Robert Schuller's Hour of Power. Dr. Schuller was a televangelist based at the Crystal Cathedral in Garden Grove, California. His was a megachurch with seating for four thousand people. At the time, the Hour of Power TV program was broadcast worldwide to about thirteen million. It's not important why I was a guest, but that day was pivotal in my career. There were two services every Sunday and after the second, Dr. Schuller invited me back to his office for a cup of coffee.*
>
> *"You were very good out there!" he said. "You should think about being a professional speaker!"*
>
> *Huh? A professional speaker? Get paid to speak? I had no idea you could do that.*

He laughed, "Oh yes, you can get paid very well to speak to corporations and conferences!"

"But how do you find people to hire you?"

Now here I was, a marketing specialist, asking for marketing advice. I should have known better, but his answer was awesome.

"Well, how do you hunt moose?"

Huh, again? I was definitely caught off-guard.

Dr. Schuller laughed and went on. "Well, you wouldn't go to Florida to hunt moose would you? No! You'd go farther north, maybe into Canada. You'd look for a forest where moose lived—where a lot of moose lived. And would you attract moose with Hostess Ding Dongs? No! You'd use some kind of moose bait, something moose would love to get and none of the other animals cared about. And would you capture a moose with a tennis racquet? No! You'd need some sort of moose gun. A big gun that's especially made for an animal the size of a moose.

"But the most important thing to understand is you're hunting moose! That's first. There are a lot of animals in the forest—bears, wild turkeys, otters, maybe big cats, birds, and fish in the streams—but you aren't interested in any of those other animals. You are only interested in moose."

Steve goes on to explain that a "Moose Strategy" is the foundation for developing an Uncopyable attachment with customers. Too many companies (and too many salespeople) assume everyone needs their product. That way of thinking is inefficient at best.

Personally, the only kind of hunting I do is for shoes. But the moose analogy is powerful. If your ideal customer is a moose, bagging a rabbit or a bear doesn't help you. Bagging the wrong prospect wastes time—your biggest asset. It also leads to unnecessary rejection—a big "ouch" for us salespeople.

Be Laser-Beam Focused

I didn't learn the term "hunting Moose" until I met Steve, but I learned the importance of the Moose Strategy during one of my college jobs. I held various hourly jobs during the summer—from waitressing (I dropped a lot of plates) to temporary office work (it put me to sleep). The most fun, and profitable, was working at Macy's the summer of my sophomore year.

When I heard Macy's was hiring sales associates for their women's department, I knew I'd be the perfect fit (pun intended). In those days, clothes shopping was my specialty. With this job, I'd be in my wheel-house. Even better, I'd earn a commission! This would be more fruitful than my minimum-wage jobs. I applied and got an interview with the department manager, Deborah.

"Each sale will be keyed in under your number," Deborah explained. As visions of dollar signs danced in my head, she continued: "At the end of the week, the sales rankings will be posted. If you're in the bottom half three weeks in a row, you're put on probation. If your sales don't pick up, I'm sorry, but you'll be laid off."

Harsh, I thought. *Heads are gonna roll.* I wasn't worried.

On the first day, I hit the department floor enthusiastically. I greeted customers who wandered into the department, helping them find things to try on. I got them different sizes, flattered them with compliments, and suggested add-ons. Basically, I did all the things I'd observed as a buyer.

I had a full week of sales under my belt when I heard the sales numbers were out. I walked into the break room with confidence. I looked up at the wall where the sales rankings were posted. My stomach lurched—my name was at the bottom.

Whaaaaat????

I tried to work harder, but at the end of week two, the result wasn't much better. Ugh. My eyes scrolled to the top of the list. I saw the same name I'd seen the week before: *Julie.*

Julie was nice. But unlike me, Julie was quiet and a bit serious. I figured my outgoing personality, wit, and charm (not to mention humility) should've given me an advantage!

She's kicking my butt, I realized.

What was I missing? I decided to shadow her. I followed her surreptitiously, peering across the department through clothes racks. It didn't take long for me to realize what she was doing. I hadn't heard the phrase at the time, but now I know: *Julie was hunting Moose.*

I'd been flitting through the department, offering to help everyone who wandered by. Julie was going for the buyers. I was wasting my time on browsers and "lookie-loos." Not Julie. She looked for only the customers who were going to buy. Once I figured that out, it was easy to spot them: their arms were full of clothes.

When she saw a customer, Julie would smile and say "hello." But she didn't actually offer to help until they'd already picked out some clothes. Then she'd spring into action. She offered to get a fitting room. She spent time helping them and giving great service—because she knew they were buyers.

In other words, they were her Moose.

As soon as I caught on, I started to make more sales. For the rest of the summer, Julie and I duked it out for the top spot.

Define Your Moose

As an Uncopyable salesperson, you're going to deliver a unique experience that will make customers *want* to buy from you. You need an effective strategy for targeting the right customers, the ones that will maximize your sales and set you both up for a win-win.

What's the profile of your Moose?

At the company level, that might include:

- Size, volume, number of locations

- Business type

- Potential to buy additional products

- Area they serve

- Family owned or corporate

- Access to the decision-maker

- An established, financially solid business

For an individual prospect, that might include:

- Professional position

- Income bracket

- Single/married/kids/no kids

- Geographic location

- Power to make a decision

- Level of influence

- Biggest challenges

- Goals and aspirations

- Age/career stage (early, middle, or ready to retire)

- Interests

- Network

For business/company prospects, a great place to start is by analyzing current customers. Then, think about the ones you want to work with. As you think about your customers and prospects, ask yourself:

- Who are my best customers?

- Which customers have had the best success with the solution I provide?

- Where do they hang out?

- Which of my customers have become raving fans?

- Who is the easiest to work with? Who's the most fun?

- With whom have I developed the best relationships?

- Who can I serve the best with my product or service?

- How long have they been in business?

- Are they buying this product or service now? Are they similar to other customers who are happily using their products?

- Are they a business I am comfortable working with?

- Do they make decisions by committee or is there a single decision-maker?

- Are they likely to want my product on an ongoing basis? *(Your existing customers are often the best prospects.)*

- What's their reputation?

- Who are my competition's best customers?

You might not sell to companies. Maybe you're looking to build your team, gig, or solo business. In this case, you're looking for an individual consumer prospect. Here are examples of some criteria for them:

- What's their family income bracket?

- What is their relationship status?

- What is their age?

- Do they have children? If so, how many?

- What is their home location?

- What are their hobbies?

- What are their affiliations (church, clubs, etc.)?

- Are they part of one or more online networks (social media, groups, etc.)?

- Are they satisfied or searching?

- Do they have an interest in generating new income?

Determine if Your Moose Acknowledges a Need

Next, determine if your Moose acknowledges a need—not necessarily for your product, but for the solution (or benefit) you're providing.

This is VERY important:

People don't change unless they are dissatisfied with the way things are right now.

Do you solve a problem? If they don't think they have that problem, if they aren't dissatisfied, you won't make the sale.

My dad was a smoker for years, and even though I begged him to quit, he wouldn't. He didn't want to—he didn't have an acknowledged need…

…until I got pregnant. When my dad became a grandpa, he stopped immediately and never picked up another cigarette. He now had an acknowledged need—and was dissatisfied with smoking. He didn't want to expose me to smoke during my pregnancy, and he didn't want to expose his first grandchild after she was born. Kelly and Grandpa celebrate that anniversary every year!

You might think your customer needs your product. Heck, you might think everyone does. But in order to make a change, your customer has to agree. At Macy's, it was pretty obvious. Customers with an armful of clothes had an acknowledged need. They were the buyers. Empty arms usually meant they were just looking.

Your job is to find prospects who are either a) already dissatisfied or b) open to new solutions to make their business or life better. In this case, the acknowledged need isn't necessarily for your product or service but for the transformation your solution represents.

One of my good friends, Patty, works in direct sales and recently expressed her frustration about one of her clients. She told me about one of her customers, who is a huge fan of the health product she sells. "She uses a ton of our products!" Patty said. "She loves the results, too. She feels so much better—the difference is night and day." There's a problem, though. Her customer loves using the products, but she isn't motivated to get involved with the business-building side. Patty told me, "I'm not going to give up! She'd be perfect for this!"

That's a sale that's almost impossible to make. Convincing a Moose who doesn't acknowledge a need wastes time that could be spent on customers who are much more receptive and a lot easier to sell. I suggested to Patty that she put her efforts into finding new Moose, ones that would be interested not only in the product, but possibly in the business opportunity as well.

I recommended two tactics:

First, instead of trying to convince her customer to pursue the opportunity (a losing and time-wasting battle), find out who her CUSTOMER knows who might be interested in her products (and maybe the business opportunity). Second, get a testimonial and ask for people Patty could contact. The result? Patty got a list of new connections, along with a glowing testimonial from her customer.

Bottom line: Be willing to walk away. Don't beat your head against the wall with the wrong prospect.

I vaguely remember my economics course from college (actually, I vaguely remember college). One economics principle that stood out is the concept of opportunity cost, which the *New Oxford American Dictionary* defines as "the loss of potential gain from other alternatives when one alternative is chosen."[5] Basically, it means that whatever you're doing right now is keeping you from doing something else.

In sales, if you're spending time on the wrong prospect, it's keeping you from pursuing another prospect, one who is much more likely to buy. To win at sales, it's critical that you don't waste time on the wrong prospect. Instead, move on to someone who will help you get the results you want. Sales is a numbers game. As soon as you find out a Moose isn't truly qualified or doesn't acknowledge a need, it's time to move on. Always ask yourself, "Is this the best use of my time?" (By the way, since right now you're reading this book, the answer is YES!)

Once You Find Moose, Cull Them Down to the Big, Hungry Moose

When I won my Territory of the Year Award with Walker, I did it by helping key customers buy more and adding large-volume customers that made a big impact on my sales. Don't waste time looking for low-potential prospects. Think strategically. Boost your sales by finding and nurturing prospects that will bring the biggest return.

Your Customers Are Also Your Moose

Think about your current customers. They're often your best prospects. They fit your profile. You've already developed a relationship with them. They've not only acknowledged a need; they've also said "yes."

Peter Drucker, the godfather of management theory, defined the purpose of business as creating a customer.[6] I agree, but I think it should be expanded to this:

The purpose of business is to create, maintain, and grow a customer.

Once we create a customer, we want to keep them as a customer, right? We don't want to have to replace everybody! We want them to keep buying from us. We want them to place more orders. We want them to place bigger orders, more often. Not only that—we want them to talk about us to other Moose!

Your goal as an Uncopyable salesperson is to become a trusted advisor. Once you've achieved that status with a customer, you can present other products or opportunities that solve additional problems or fulfill aspirations. With each customer, ask yourself, "What else?" Just like a waiter who suggests appetizers and dessert when you order dinner, find ways to offer to your customer more, now and in the future.

Know Your Moose Better Than the Competition

Knowing your Moose better than the competition is an Uncopyable secret. Once you target your Moose, gather information that will help you with the next steps in the sales process.

Google

It's amazing (and a little scary) how much information about a person or company you can find online. This is your advantage as an Uncopyable salesperson. A Google search can uncover information you didn't know about. You might find newspapers, journals, articles, or blog posts your prospect has written. You can find reviews, BBB complaints, or other clues about your prospect. If you want to go further, set up a Google alert and get daily updates on anything published about the company.

Company Websites

Look at the company's website. Learn what you can about the company—from their mission and positioning to the products and services they provide. You can find helpful information on how they position themselves by seeing how they explain what they do. If they have a newsletter or ask for your email, sign up! You never know what they'll share. Learn about their philosophy. Finally, look at their website from their customer's point of view. If possible, drill down to uncover *their* customer's pain points—the ones they're working to solve.

Social Media

Most people's LinkedIn profiles give their work history, education, and schools they attended. They might also list interests, endorsements, and even volunteer activities. You could find you have mutual connections.

It's also worth looking them up on Facebook, Twitter, and Instagram. And who knows what other social media might pop up? As I'm writing this, TikTok is growing rapidly, and by the time you read this, there will most likely be other new ones. If your prospect uses any of these platforms, they'll help you get more personal information. Remember, you're looking for places your Moose is hanging out!

Personal Networking

More and more of what we do has moved online, but that doesn't mean personal networking is defunct or less important. If you want to approach a prospective client, talking to someone who has worked with that person or company can be extremely valuable. Not only can you find out information about the prospect that can be very helpful in putting together your Uncopyable sales strategy, but having a mutual acquaintance introduce you is a huge advantage.

BONUS CONTENT AND WORKBOOK AVAILABLE AT

UNCOPYABLESALES.COM/RESOURCES

SECTION TWO

ENGAGEMENT

CHAPTER 5

YOU'VE GOT TO
GET IN THE DOOR!

My cell phone rang. It was my friend and ski buddy Trudy, and boy was she excited:

"GUESS WHO CALLED ME??"

Trudy is a sales rep for Valpak, an advertising program for local businesses. A few months before, she'd vented her frustration on the way to ski at Crystal Mountain. "I have a prospect—an automotive repair business," she said. "I think our advertising campaign would be perfect for them. But I can't get in the door!"

It's not like she hadn't tried. She called. The gatekeepers transferred her to voicemail. She sent emails. No response. She stopped by several times and left her card. Nothing. Zip. Nada.

I suggested a tactic I've personally used many times to get the owner's attention. "Try it. I bet he'll take your call. What have you got to lose?"

She took my advice, leading to the result you already read: "GUESS WHO CALLED ME??"

What did Trudy do? Trudy used good, old-fashioned direct mail but with a high-tech, digital twist we've been using for 15 years. She sent a personalized greeting card. It took her only a few minutes to create, and her cost was less than two bucks.

"The owner called ME," she said. He told her she got his attention. Trudy set an appointment. A couple meetings later, he signed an agreement for an ongoing campaign.

Get in the Door can mean different things. You might not be literally trying to get in the door, but you do need to stand out and connect. This is critical, because before anything else happens, you need to get on the prospect's radar!

In chapter 4, I talked about the importance of defining your Moose. Your Moose is the focus of your sales efforts because they're the most likely to buy and benefit from your product or service. Guess what? Your Moose is likely your competition's Moose, too. Not only that— your prospect might be happy with whatever they're doing, seeing it as "good enough." Either way, you need to grab their attention.

Most salespeople approach prospects the same way. They use phone and email—or sometimes make a cold call. Buyers used to have physical gatekeepers. Voicemail and email have become the new gatekeepers. "Leave a message," the recorded greeting says. Expecting a call back is a pipe dream. What about email? Look at the flood of emails in your inbox. Do you return emails from people you don't know?

If you want an Uncopyable advantage, make engaging your Moose your focus from the start. Your first contact with a prospect is the foundation of your sales relationship. It's also your first impression. To be different, walk your talk...from the beginning.

LOOK AT WHAT
EVERYONE ELSE
IS DOING, AND
DON'T DO IT.

Too many salespeople fall into the same communication traps. First, they send an email like this:

> *Hello Kay Miller,*
>
> *I hope this email finds you and your team in good health!*
>
> *I would love to share with you how I've helped my clients surpass their competition thanks to distinct messaging. Would you be open to discovering how it could work for you? If so, you can reserve a free consultation here: https:// calendly.com/fardeldarkusmarketing.*
>
> *I look forward to talking with you soon!*
>
> *Sincerely,*
>
> *Cynthia Fardeldarkus*

Wow, if I received this, I would IMMEDIATELY set an appointment! Wouldn't you?

NOT.

When that message doesn't work, they might try calling. Of course, they just get voicemail, so they essentially leave the exact same message as their email.

And salespeople wonder why they can't get the appointment. Sigh…

We MUST get in the door! But in today's world, that takes creativity.

How do you do that?

The Next Step

Years ago, we developed a philosophy we call "Next Step."

Next Step keeps sales and marketing campaigns on a very simple path. Regardless of where you are in the relationship-building process—whether you're on the very first communication or the sixth—what's the very next step that needs to happen?

If you send something in the mail, your goal is to get it opened. If you send an email broadcast, the very next step is getting the recipients to OPEN the email! That's it. If they don't open the email, it doesn't matter how amazing your message is. That makes the subject line extremely important.

Once they open the email, don't jump into a sales pitch. Come up with a low-risk next step for them to take—one that provides useful and interesting value to them. Maybe a free report they can download. If that's the next step, then your messaging is designed to get the reader to take that action. Nothing more. Don't write about your company being established in 1987. Don't tell them to call for a quote. Stay 100 percent focused on the next step.

Here are some tried-and-true Next Step strategies to get in the door. They've worked for me, and they've worked for our clients. Use these secrets to make an Uncopyable impression from the start and get in the door!

Send a Personalized Greeting Card

This is the strategy Trudy used: she sent a personalized greeting card. Her prospect was so impressed that he picked up the phone and immediately called her.

Of course, this wasn't just any greeting card. This one was unique: on the front of the card was *his picture* with the caption "I want to meet with YOU!"

Imagine opening a 5x7 envelope that's personally addressed to you and seeing your own lovely mug staring back. Talk about an attention grabber!

I asked where she found his photo. "It was easy," Trudy said. She found it on Facebook. Because they had some mutual connections, she could access his photos. Not everyone is on Facebook. But his picture was also on LinkedIn and on the company website.

On the inside, she wrote, "Hi, I'm Trudy Miller. You obviously have a successful business. I've done some digging, and I believe there's even more business out there. I'd like to get to know you and see if we can work together to capture it. Would you be willing to meet?"

Then she made a joke: "You have awesome gatekeepers!" she said.

Trudy created the card using an online service that makes it easy to design and send personalized cards, one at a time. The card design that's been the most successful for me is to use the prospect's photo on the front and frame it with a "wanted poster." (The frame is easy to find online.) Whenever I do that, people enjoy the joke. I've gotten appointments (that have led to sales) when nothing else worked. As Trudy put it, "Using the card as an introduction set the tone for a different kind of relationship." Based on Trudy's card, plus her follow-ups, the owner committed to an ongoing advertising program. Since then, Trudy has helped him measurably grow his business, targeting the geographical areas and market segments he'd been missing. When she told me the story, she added, "He's become one of my favorite customers."

For Trudy, the card was the start of a beautiful friendship. She not only made a personal connection, but her new customer also said she showed creativity and persistence—proving she's a different kind of salesperson.

Send Lumpy Mail

Basically, lumpy mail has something inside that piques your prospect's curiosity. They know something is inside the envelope. They can't resist peeking to find out.

When Steve and I launched our speaking and consulting business, we decided to target the trade show industry. I started by sending what we called "sugar daddy" mailings. My goal was to get in the door with the associations and management companies who organized and ran trade shows. These became my Moose.

Trade shows are a huge revenue source. Most exhibitors treated these shows as necessary but expensive evils, so we studied them carefully and interviewed a lot of buyers. Then we developed a strategy that turned exhibiting from a high line-item expense into a real investment with measurable ROI. We also helped the associations and management companies that produce trade shows make even more money.

Once we determined the specific Moose that made the most sense, we planned a marketing campaign. Our mailings focused on one of their acknowledged pains: exhibitors blame the trade show management when they don't get the results they want. When that happens, the exhibitors don't come back. It's a big blow to the trade show's revenue stream. That churn forces them to grind each year to find replacement exhibitors.

In the "sugar daddy" mailing, I included a brief letter. "Do you feel like a sugar daddy to your exhibitors?" the headline read.

In addition, I included a response form with a valuable call to action offering a free 45-minute recorded presentation. (If you know anything about the Uncopyable philosophy, you know every marketing message needs a call to action.) We had a 46 percent response on the initial mailing! Those envelopes got opened because the prospects who received them wanted to know what was inside. They responded, too—because we were offering something of value to them. They became qualified prospects. Reaching out to those qualified prospects became the first step of my sales process. Dealing with prospects who had responded and expressed interest gave me a huge advantage in making sales.

Send a "Shock and Awe" Package

One of the most impressive and effective direct marketing strategies you can use to stand out to new prospects is a "shock and awe" package. A "shock and awe" package is designed to do exactly what it says. You want it to be unlike anything else your customer gets.

Our "shock and awe" packages are, no surprise, ORANGE. Completely orange. From the packaging, to the color ink we use, to what goes inside. It's consistent with our brand color and stands out because of it.

The power of a "shock and awe" package has been proven. After sending one, a prospect I'd been trying to reach called *me* and said, "In all my years in this business, I've never gotten anything like this!"

Her name was Amanda, and she was the decision-maker in an organization that fit the criteria of my Moose perfectly. I'd sent a lumpy mailing that included a call to action. No response. I followed up by email and phone to no avail.

Three days later, Amanda received a package—a large, orange "shock and awe" box. When she opened the box, she was greeted with a "grab bag" of very cool gifts, each carefully wrapped (by yours truly) in bright orange tissue paper. Amanda went through the box, unwrapping each item: an autographed copy of *Uncopyable*, a blank journal, an umbrella, a moose shot glass, and a "moose whistle." All were bright orange. When she came to the signature sunglasses we send our customers (the frame and lenses are both bright orange), she saw not one pair but THREE. She read the attached note: "For your kids." (I'd done some sleuthing and knew she had two!)

That's when she picked up the phone and told me how much it impressed her.

Through a few more conversations and follow-ups, we got to know each other. When the time was right, I made a recommendation for a consulting project and sent her a proposal based on delivering the exact solution she was looking for. She said "yes"! I never would have made that sale if I hadn't sent a "shock and awe" package.

Send Video Brochures or Custom Videos

Video brochures merge the physical and the digital. They're about the size of an old VCR cassette (if you remember such a thing). The video brochure acts as the video "player." As soon as it's opened, your video starts to play.

One of our clients has used these with great results. Email a video link for a customer to view and there's little chance they'll watch it. Send them a physical player, where the video plays on opening, and it's a different story. (Google "video brochures" and you'll find lots of options. The cost is less than you might think.)

Custom videos can also help grab your prospect's attention enough for them to listen to your pitch, as well as strengthen existing client relationships. Early in the pandemic, we developed an "empathy marketing campaign." As part of our campaign, we hired Tom Bergeron (of *America's Funniest Home Videos* and *Dancing with the Stars* fame) to record a personal, inspirational video for our BFFs (that's what we call our friends and followers). Bergeron delivered a warm, genuine, and FUNNY message. It was a big hit, and we got a ton of great feedback. It was a great way to connect with both prospects and customers in a fun and positive way. It not only got us in the door with new prospects, but it was also a really efficient way to solidify our existing relationships.

Tips for sending or delivering something useful and interesting:

- Send a book you think will help their business or them professionally

- Send white papers

- Send case studies

- Send something that has to do with THEM. I heard one example of someone who found out their prospect had a beloved dog that was his pride and joy. The person sent a customized dog collar and some dog treats. WOW! Another sent a hat from the prospect's alma mater (it's easy to get that info on LinkedIn).

- Send a sample, but do it creatively. One of our clients, Coni Lefferts, is the president of a custom packaging company, Creative Packaging Solutions. Her company sends product samples to qualified prospects and customers so they can see and experience the quality of the product for themselves. She mentioned that she always has her team wrap samples in brightly colored tissue paper. I asked Coni how she came up with the idea. "From my own experience!" she said. She told me about the time she requested samples from one of her vendors. They arrived in a plain cardboard box—loose and rolling around like they'd been carelessly thrown together. It made a bad impression. Because of that, every sample they send is carefully wrapped and makes a completely different, and noticeable, impression.

Samples work well if you can find an opportunity to offer them. We use a health product we buy from our Pilates teacher, Crystal. Before we tried it, Crystal had mentioned it, but we weren't that interested. Then she dropped off a sample. We loved it—and became ongoing customers! If you can, send a sample of your product—or better yet, do what Crystal did: deliver it yourself!

For an even bigger impact, put what you send in a shiny envelope or colored box.

Use UPS or FedEx to deliver it. (If you want somebody to spend thousands of dollars with you, don't be cheap on shipping costs!)

Do Something Out of Left Field

One of our consulting clients is a successful truck equipment company called Zoresco. The company is family owned and values based. Take a look at their website (zoresco.com), and you'll immediately see a focus on great relationships with customers and an extreme commitment to their customers' success.

During Christmas 2020, in the middle of the COVID-19 pandemic, Zoresco wanted to do something unusual and Uncopyable for their customers and big prospects. The salespeople hand-delivered full-sized, red Radio Flyer wagons—which tied into the quality their company delivers, as well as the company color. I talked to Nick Costa, one of their salespeople. "It gave me access to prospects I'd never been able to connect with," he told me. Once they got to know him, some were willing to schedule a meeting. Nick was able to learn more about them and develop a relationship. When the time was right, he recommended a next step (such as taking Zoresco's free assessment) and ended up making new sales.

"Not only did it connect me with some great prospects," Nick told me, "it helped me figure out which prospects weren't actually my Moose. It saved me from wasting time with the wrong prospects." Nick was able to say, "NEXT!" and move on to his actual Moose.

(Nick also told me a funny story about one prospect who declined the Radio Flyer. "We can't accept gifts," the prospect said. Nick replied, "It's not a gift; it's a marketing piece!" They kept the wagon.)

In addition, Zoresco offered something even more unique—a series of webinars to provide value. That value was not only aimed at their current customers. It also targeted, as the sales manager put it, "our future customers." But these weren't the usual "here's what we have to sell to you" online presentations. With our help, Zoresco hired two best-selling authors, Eliz Greene and Sam Silverstein, to do interviews for special webinars. Eliz talked about managing stress during COVID, and Sam spoke about the pandemic's effect on leadership. Neither of these webinars were directly connected with Zoresco's products, but they provided useful and interesting information. Their Moose were impressed!

Like the Radio Flyer wagons, the webinars helped Zoresco's sales-people make headway with prospects they hadn't been able to reach before—even after years of trying. Some of those prospects signed up for the webinars, giving them the opening they needed. "It not only got me in the door," Nick said, "it changed the conversation."

What can you do to provide prospects with value up front? What can you share—beyond your normal product communications? This is your opportunity to prove to *future* customers, as Zoresco calls them, that you care. Look for ways to prove that you're committed to making their business and/or life better—beyond just making the sale.

Don't Just Break the Rules— Change the Game

"No Soliciting" signs keep other salespeople out. If you have the guts to ignore them, you have an advantage. The thing is, when you see one of those, you have to tell yourself you probably won't get in. Getting rejected doesn't hurt as much when it's what you expect! But a lot of other times, I've found the sign works to "thin the herd." Ignoring them is an example of how breaking the rules can give YOU the advantage.

One of our clients did something even gutsier when she called on a prospect. She works for company that provides temporary office help. She walked into the office of a prospect, and there was nobody there. There was a receptionist's desk, but it was empty. Next to the desk was a door marked "Private." She asked herself, *What have I got to lose?* She knocked on the door. A beat of silence followed. Then she heard a voice: "Come in."

She apologized for intruding but said she'd like to talk to the owner for a moment. Sure enough, she'd found him. He chuckled, then said, "Sit down." She was rewarded by not only making a sale—she earned the business of a loyal and repeat customer.

Another one of our clients has changed the rules by disrupting the "always be closing" mentality in sales. (Remember the famous scene in *Glengarry Glen Ross* where Alec Baldwin's character attacks the sales team repeatedly with "Always Be Closing"—"ABC"?!)

Obviously you want to make sales. But again, people don't want to be sold, manipulated, or pushed. Here's an example of a salesperson whose sales have skyrocketed by *not* constantly pushing for the close.

Earlier, I talked about Nick Costa of Zoresco, who delivered Radio Flyer wagons to new prospects during the holidays. You might have wondered what happened next. (Either way, you're about to find out!)

Nick didn't stop there. He'd always tried to be more than "just a salesperson," but in the past year, he's taken his approach with prospects and customers to the next level. The shift was intentional, but it was accelerated by supply chain issues prevalent during the COVID-19 pandemic. Now, his primary role is to truly be a *resource*.

"Whether they're customers or not, if they have a question, a problem, or a part they can't find, I tell them, 'Call me.'" If he can't help,

Nick uses his connections and does his best to find someone who can. He recently helped a fleet manager find 15 utility trucks they couldn't find anywhere else. He helped the customer out of a real bind—even though it wasn't a sale.

Because of his actions, his network has exploded. Customers and prospects are calling *him*. His fleet manager customers are recommending him to both their end users as well as their peers. One of Nick's fleet management customers is working to get him into multiple locations in other parts of the country.

Nick has built an Uncopyable reputation. "I'm getting multiple calls every day. I'll pick up the phone, and they'll say, 'I have a problem, and I was told to "Call Nick!"'"

This is the opposite of an adversarial relationship, where one party is trying to talk the other person into doing, or buying, something they don't necessarily want. It goes far beyond being a "closer," or "handling" objections. Nick has become a valuable resource, and his sales reflect the change.

When I asked him about the results of his new approach, he answered, "I'm ecstatic." It has made the sales process—and the relationships—much more gratifying. And yes, it's translating into MORE SALES. When we talked, he told me about a big sale he'd just made to a buyer who was referred to him because of his reputation. "It's so much more fun than cold calling—and a heck of a lot more profitable," he said. "I'm enjoying this new role as a 'resource' more than I ever enjoyed 'just' being a salesperson."

When it comes to building a sales relationship, nothing else happens until you get in the door. And oftentimes, getting in the door looks different than simply scheduling a sales presentation. It can mean getting on the prospect's radar and piquing their interest by building a reputation of service and always seeking connection over and above "the close." This step is one of the biggest challenges for salespeople—because most of them use the same worn-out tactics.

Set your sights on making a first impression and using a sales approach that prove you're different. You'll not only have more success connecting with your Moose, but you'll also build an Uncopyable reputation. Who knows—they may be so impressed, they'll call YOU!

You're invited to use the ideas in this chapter—they're tried and true yet still unique. I also encourage you to expand on them. Use your own creativity to grab the attention of your prospect. Make a first impression that's original and establishes you as the kind of person who doesn't think or act like everyone else. In other words, show them that YOU are the kind of person they want to do business with.

BONUS CONTENT AND WORKBOOK AVAILABLE AT
UNCOPYABLESALES.COM/RESOURCES

CHAPTER 6

DEVELOP A MUTUALLY TRUSTING RELATIONSHIP

"I'll never do business with Walker again!"

Those were the words that started one of my favorite customer relationships. The relationship—with Jerry Cornell of Cornell Auto Parts—was special because it started out on such a rocky road.

I first heard about Cornell Auto Parts during my last round of job interviews with Walker. I was at the home office in Racine, Wisconsin. (The trip was memorable because I was introduced to Kringles, a local, to-die-for confectionery.) I was at headquarters for the approval of the bigwigs. One of them was Frank Grosser, the VP of sales. "Kay," he said, "if we hire you, you have to promise you'll win back Cornell Auto Parts."

Frank didn't have all the details, but something had gone wrong. Jerry Cornell, the owner of an important northwest distributor, had sent him a letter. In it, he swore he'd never do business with the company again.

After I was hired, I called my district manager, Dennis. "What happened?" I inquired. Dennis filled me in. A big Walker shipment had been delayed because of a backorder issue. Even worse, the former rep—the one I replaced—didn't tell the customer. Jerry was beyond ticked. He dropped the Walker line and replaced it with a different one.

Cornell Auto Parts was located in Port Angeles, way up in the northwest corner of Washington State. (Fun fact: It's close to the town of Forks, later made famous as the setting for the popular Twilight books and movies.) Compared to our other distributors, Cornell was small. But it was critically important, because the company supplied an area none of our other distributors covered.

I called Jerry and introduced myself. "Hi, Mr. Cornell, I'm Kay Miller—the new territory manager for Walker. I heard there was a problem. Would you be willing to meet so you can tell me what happened?"

"It won't do you any good," Jerry said. "I'll never buy from Walker again."

"I get it. But I'll be in the area...can I at least stop by?"

Actually, I was going to the area specifically to see HIM. He might have guessed that. Either way, he agreed to a date and time.

I drove to Port Angeles the night before our appointment and stayed at a hotel. It was a long drive—I couldn't risk being late. When I got to the warehouse the next morning, Jerry was standing next to the counter, talking to a customer. I listened in. I could tell he was a good guy.

It took a while for them to finish. I'm pretty sure Jerry drew out the conversation just to make me wait. *Fair enough*, I thought. When the customer left, he gruffly pointed to his office. He motioned to a chair, then sat at his desk and crossed his arms.

I sat down, leaned forward, and said, "I understand you had a problem."

Jerry made a face. "It was a nightmare."

"What happened?" I genuinely wanted to know.

"Your predecessor screwed up. My shipment didn't come. When I figured out something was wrong, I called him. He didn't bother to call me back."

I pulled out a small pad of paper and jotted down some notes.

"I lost business," he continued. "My customers lost business. Not only that—it made me look bad. My reputation is *everything*."

We'd lost Jerry's trust, and I knew it would take a long time to get it back again.

When he finally ran out of steam, I looked him in the eye and said, "I'm sorry. I promise that won't happen again."

I told him I admired his commitment to his customers, because I did. I understood how upsetting it was for him to let his customers down. I said I couldn't imagine how frustrating that experience must have been.

If he gave me the opportunity to prove myself, I promised he'd have up-to-date information on every order. He'd know right away if something went wrong. "If there's a problem, you'll be covered—whether it's with fill-in inventory from one of our Seattle warehouses, or even the competition."

"We'll see," he said. It took a while, but eventually, Jerry brought our line back into his warehouse. The day he placed the full restocking order was a proud moment. Word got back to Frank Grosser. I still have the personal letter of congratulations he sent me!

To this day, I'm convinced that active *listening* was the only way to save his account. If I'd started out by talking, I'd have lost the chance to win Cornell's business back. If I'd argued, been defensive, or disagreed with him, he wouldn't have changed his mind. Active listening saved the day, and I recommend you use this powerful tool in every business conversation you have.

Active Listening— Your Uncopyable Superpower

Active listening involves going beyond just hearing what your counter-part is saying. It means you:

- Listen with your ears
- Observe with your eyes
- Strive to understand

Listen with Your Ears

Salespeople like to talk. Heck, most people do! And guess what our favorite subject is? Ourselves, of course. We want to talk about what's most important: our lives, our opinions, our beliefs, our families, our accomplishments, where we've been, and what we've bought. When someone listens to us, asks questions, and wants to know more, we're drawn to that person like the proverbial moth to a flame.

The need to listen might seem obvious, but...

A few weeks ago, my friend Cheryl called me. She had friends coming to town for a visit, and they were going to stay overnight. "I took a look around my house," she said. "This place is a mess!"

She was exaggerating—her place is never a mess. But I totally got it. When "company is coming," as people used to say, all of a sudden you look around with fresh eyes. You see the trouble spots you've blissfully ignored.

In Cheryl's case, the problem was moss. Thanks to our damp northwest climate (we don't tan; we rust!) the green slimy stuff covered her driveway and the path to her front door. She wanted it gone. She looked online for home maintenance companies that did power washing. She picked two and called for estimates.

The first company she contacted was "Power Wash Dudes." (That's not the real company name. I don't want to throw the real business under the bus.)

The owner and main Power Wash Dude said he could come out the next morning to take a look. They agreed on a time.

Cheryl called me the next day, after he left. It hadn't gone well.

"Geez. Power Wash Dude showed up with a *three-ring binder.* He sat at my dining room table for a HALF HOUR and went through his entire presentation. He told me everything—right down to "The 3 Ps of Power Washing."

"Ick," I said. "What *are* the 3 Ps of Power Washing?"

"I have no idea. I was so bored; all I could think about was when he was going to leave."

Power Wash Dude clearly believed in his service. He gave Cheryl a plethora of details to prove he'd do an outstanding job. But he didn't stand a chance of selling her. He couldn't have convinced her because he didn't listen. The bottom line? Your customer doesn't care about you; they care about what you can do for *them*.

Don't get me wrong—it's important to be enthusiastic about your product, service, or solution. As salespeople, we're selling something we believe in. We know how awesome it is. Hey, we've drunk the Kool-Aid! But to persuade someone, we need to make it about *them*. We need to put ourselves in the customer's shoes and find out what we can to uncover their problem or aspiration.

None of that is possible unless you listen first.

"Make me feel important."

That's what Jim Reiman, one of our clients, said. Jim owns a successful business called Tropic Waters Pet Center in Eau Claire, Wisconsin. As a family-owned business competing with the big box stores, he insists his employees sell only products they would use for their own pets. Jim's the one who buys all the merchandise—and has the same high standards for choosing which vendors to work with. When I asked him, "What can a salesperson do to make you want to buy from them?" Jim said the No. 1 thing a salesperson can do is to listen to him. "Too many salespeople want to do all the talking. When I meet the rare salesperson who wants to know what I have to say? That's the salesperson I want to do business with."

Listening takes a conscious effort. Remember how your mom said, "You have two ears and one mouth for a reason"? (My mom said that a lot—she knew me well.) Having the discipline to listen is one of the biggest Uncopyable sales secrets of all.

Back when I was with Walker, I took a Dale Carnegie class on "How to Win Friends and Influence People." Walker management encouraged all of us salespeople to take the class and covered the cost. I figured I'd earn some brownie points with my boss. I signed up.

The course turned out to be a lot better than I expected. I remember one particular class where the instructor told us we'd be doing role plays. The goal was to practice listening. Before we started, she told us one of the stories from Carnegie's classic book.

Carnegie was at a dinner party and found himself enthralled by a "distinguished botanist." Carnegie relays the story in the book:

> *I literally sat on the edge of my chair and listened while he spoke of exotic plants and experiments in developing new forms of plant life and indoor gardens (and even told me astonishing facts about the humble potato).*[7]

As Carnegie explained, their conversation lasted for hours. Afterward, the botanist referred to Carnegie as "a most interesting conversationalist."

"In reality," Carnegie concluded, "I had been merely a good listener and had encouraged him to talk."

When you're talking to a prospective customer, tune in to what they say. If you're on the phone, pay attention to the tone of their voice. Do they sound engaged, animated, interested? Are they giving you detailed answers? Or are they slow to respond, answering your questions with just a yes/no answer? Pay attention. How they say something is just as important—or more important—than what they say.

Observe with Your Eyes

Studying people's surroundings is one of the best secrets to building customer relationships. Look for family photos, pictures of the "big fish" they've caught, or awards they've earned.

I once called on a guy named Ray who was pretty intimidating on the phone. He hardly talked, and he'd answer my questions in the fewest words possible. His emails were the same—borderline abrupt. He was all business, and I was a little nervous about meeting him face to face.

When I went to his office, my eyes quickly darted around his surroundings. Aha! His office wall was covered with Little League plaques. He was obviously a long-time sponsor of local Little League teams. Once I got him on that subject, he turned into a real talker. Tuning into Ray's surroundings gave me all I needed to get him to open up.

That kind of "intel" is one of the reasons I like video calls over phone calls whenever I have the choice. Besides reading the other person's body language, a video call gives you a peek into their environment. Is there a bookshelf? What's on it? Why did they select those specific items? Are there family photos? Even if they use a virtual background, you could ask why they chose that particular one (as long as it's not a generic office scene)! There might not always be a story, but when there is, you get valuable information.

In addition to observing someone's environment, you can observe their body language. This works best when the meeting is face to face, but you can also study body language on video calls. When I observe someone's body language, I like to pretend I'm one of those palm readers you might see at a carnival or fair.

The annual Seattle Fremont Street Fair and Solstice Parade is legendary. I went with a group of friends once. There were vendors of all kinds, and just for fun, I decided to pay a psychic to read my palms. Call me a skeptic—I didn't believe my palm wrinkles could predict my future. But I'd never done it before and figured it would be entertaining.

It was. What fascinated me the most was the palm reader's performance. After I paid my money and sat down, she composed herself, smoothing her dress and clearing a space on her small table. She gently reached for my hand. As she turned it over, she looked not at my palm, but at my eyes. I could tell she was totally tuned in. She started with pleasantries and then launched into "the reading." I realized that when she'd start to say something, she'd watch for my reaction. "I see a sister..." she'd begin. But my face told her that wasn't quite right. She noticed the slightest movement of my face or body and would quickly correct herself. "I mean a brother..."

The whole time, I watched her in awe. She was truly a master at reading body language.

I've always thought of that palm reader when I look for nonverbal clues in a sales situation. Cheryl's description of Power Wash Dude was the complete opposite of the palm reader. Power Wash Dude paid no attention to her nonverbal cues. I could imagine how uncomfortable she must have been—fidgeting, breaking eye contact, watching the clock. He wasn't tuned in to Cheryl.

Don't make that mistake. Be sure to watch closely for body language cues!

Strive to Understand

Active listening is more than keeping your mouth shut. You want to *show* you're interested in what they're saying. Your own nonverbal cues send powerful messages.

When most people listen, they're waiting for their turn to talk. They're forming their response in their mind. They can't wait to share their own perspective on the subject. Again, in a sales relationship, make it about them. Then, become a human sponge for what they tell you! Do that, and you'll have a huge advantage over your competition. To excel at active listening:

- **Make eye contact.** It's important to look at the other person when talking. But take cues from the other person...don't drill holes in their head. Find what's comfortable. Looking up or away is fine, but make sure they know from your eyes that you're focused on them. Lean slightly forward. The key word is *slightly*—just enough to show you're interested.

- **Focus on what the other person is saying.** Avoid mentally preparing your response while the other person is talking.

- **Take notes.** I prefer taking notes on paper. This not only helps you focus, but it also sends a clear message to the buyer that you're "tuned in." (When someone takes notes on their phone, I never know if they're actually scrolling Instagram.)

- **Nod occasionally to show you're listening.** But don't overdo it.

- **Don't try to fill every silence.** A lapse in conversation is okay. Give the customer time to digest and think. Give them some room to talk.

No matter what kind of sales you're in, spend the time to actively listen to your prospect first. They'll not only appreciate it, but they'll also tell you what you need to know. When it's time to help them buy, you'll be armed with the exact information that resonates with them. You'll be in the perfect position to help them make the wisest buying decision.

The Trust Factor

We've all heard people buy from people they know, like, and trust. To me, trust is paramount in sales. No matter what the selling situation, you can't overcome a lack of trust, even if someone knows and likes you.

But how do you build trust, the critical ingredient in any long-term relationship?

I shared the various steps I took to build Jerry's trust back in my Walker days, but it took several months and many meetings with him. I had to deliver 100 percent on my promise to him in that first meeting and every time after.

How do you develop that mutually trusting relationship, or win it back again, when necessary?

Tell the Truth

I was on a sales call with my Amerock sales manager once. We were talking to a customer, and they were considering a big order. "We need it to arrive within six weeks. Can you do that?"

"Sure," my manager said.

His answer made me squirm. I knew that we were having a supply problem. We couldn't guarantee the delivery window he'd promised.

From then on, I decided that if I didn't know the answer to something, I'd say, "I don't know the answer, but I'll find out." (Admitting you don't know the answer proves you're truthful!) When you follow up with the answer, as promised, it gives you the chance to further prove you can be trusted.

Customers are smart. I'm sure you've been on the end of a sales transaction—or maybe even a conversation—where the other person is "winging it." The first time you catch someone stretching the truth—or downright lying—your trust in them is damaged. It's almost impossible to get that trust back. When my manager made that questionable delivery promise, I followed up the next day with the home office. Sure enough, we couldn't guarantee that delivery date. I immediately called the customer. "I checked on the delivery date—six weeks might be a problem. I wanted you to know right away. Let's work together on what to do just in case."

If you tell a customer you'll do something, do it. And if you tell them *when* you'll do it, that's when you do it. A good rule of thumb is to "under-promise and overdeliver." Don't tell your customer you'll do something unless you're sure you can do it when you say you will.

Trust must be built over time—and it must be built with trustworthy action. Here's a tip: I recommend you find an excuse to follow up whenever you can—or even create one. Every time you say, "I'll get back to you by Thursday," and then do it, you're building trust. Find something you can promise to get for the customer, and then do it. I'm amazed at how many times customers are impressed that I simply do what I said I would!

And if you're unable to fulfill your promise…

DO WHAT YOU SAY YOU WILL DO, AND DO IT WHEN YOU SAY YOU'RE GOING TO DO IT.

Deliver Bad News First & Fast

When something goes wrong, it's never fun. On the other hand, problems give you an opportunity. Salespeople are always happy to deliver good news. But your customer will appreciate and respect you for delivering the bad news—and delivering it quickly. The sooner they know there's a problem, the sooner they can begin to plan and prepare for it. Let them know ASAP. Assure them you'll stay on top of it, and if you can, find ways to help.

When it comes to communication, silence is definitely not golden. What if you don't have the answer you're waiting for? Don't wait to let your customer know. More communication is always better than less. A simple email telling them "No news yet" is better than silence. Your customer will appreciate it, and you'll set yourself apart from the salespeople who don't have the guts to deliver bad news.

I'll admit all this sounds like commonsense, practical, anybody-can-do-it advice.

Here's the big secret: The percentage of salespeople who follow this advice is actually pretty small. That's sad, right? Not for YOU—it's GREAT news for the Uncopyable salesperson! You have the opportunity to stand out simply by doing things other salespeople don't or won't do.

Make your customer relationships about them: Listen. Observe. Be trustworthy. Commit to these basics, and you'll build mutually trusting relationships that help you win at sales.

BONUS CONTENT AND WORKBOOK AVAILABLE AT

UNCOPYABLESALES.COM/RESOURCES

CHAPTER 7

THINK LIKE SHERLOCK HOLMES

I saw the majestic ruins of the Roman Forum in Italy from a perspective shared by few others: from the ground. I mean literally from the ground...lying on my back...in the dirt.

I was on a European trip with my best friend, Teri, and our teenage daughters. We'd been to Europe years earlier—long before we had kids. (That first trip was the one my customer generously paid for!)

On our first trip, we packed light. At the time, we were young—in our early 20s. All we needed were our backpacks, a few Rick Steves guidebooks, and our youthful sense of adventure! We bought Eurail passes and planned our destinations on the fly. During one of our train rides, we talked about the future. We imagined the husbands and kids we'd each eventually have. We made a pact: someday Teri and I would take our kids on a trip to Europe!

Fast-forward a couple decades. By then we were both married, our imaginary kids were real live teenagers, and we were on the trip we'd dreamed of (this one included a LOT of luggage). I hadn't dreamed about this part, though...

It was a searing hot August day during an unusual heat wave. We were at the Roman Forum, located below street level, requiring a trek down a long set of stairs. The sun bore down on us, its heat intense. The surrounding walls blocked any potential breeze. I looked for a place to sit, but there wasn't one. That's when I started to feel faint. *Uh oh.* My only option was to lie down.

I crumpled to the ground, drifting out of consciousness. My daughter, Kelly, raced to my side. She was worried about my welfare—and equally embarrassed. (In an unfortunate coincidence, this was the day I'd decided to wear a skirt!) Kelly made diligent efforts to keep my knees from splaying open in a very unladylike fashion.

Then...a miracle. A young Italian man walked toward me to help. Was it a mirage? No, it was Gino, the personal Italian tour guide we'd hired for the day! After giving me a few sips of water from the bottle he carried, he reached out his hand and helped me to my feet. He escorted me up the steps to the street level, with the rest of the group in tow. I followed him, bleary-eyed, as he steered us toward a café—one I hadn't noticed was there. Gino spoke a few words in Italian to the restaurant host. Soon we were sipping Limonatas in a shady spot under a tree, with a cool breeze wafting through.

It's hard to describe the relief of that moment—it was a slice of heaven. After a light lunch, we were all cooled down and feeling refreshed. For the rest of the day, Gino whisked us from one sight to another, guiding us onto the subways, hailing cabs and taking us on shortcuts through scenic side streets. He conversed easily with us in fluent English and in his native language with our various Italian hosts. He got us VIP access, leading us to the front of long lines. He procured ticket discounts. He steered us away from sights that were overrated and showed us hidden gems that weren't in the guidebooks. And—very important to our girls—he took us to the best spots for gelato!

We'd planned the rest of our mini European tour ourselves. But when it came to Rome, we'd gotten stuck. There was extra pressure because we'd promised our teenagers our Rome sightseeing would be condensed into a single day. In the midst of our frustration, Teri had a lightbulb moment. "Let's hire a personal guide."

YESSSS. She did some research and found Gino. He specialized in private, customized sightseeing tours. He was a native Italian, a history buff, and family friendly. "He's not cheap," she warned.

"You get what you pay for," I answered. He turned out to be a bargain.

When Teri reached out to Gino by email, the first thing he did was ask questions. He wanted to know everything about us and the kind of experience we had in mind.

- How many adults, teens?

- Do you want your day to be fast-paced or relaxed?

- Transportation: subway, cab, or walking?

- Are there specific sights you want to see?

- How long can you spend?

- How much walking do you want to do?

- What time should we start?

- Is a "normal" dinner time okay (9 pm?!)

- How would you describe your ideal day of Rome sightseeing?

By the time we met Gino, he'd planned the whole day based on what he'd learned about us.

The morning of our tour, we set off on an itinerary geared toward two moms and three teens with minimal attention spans and limited interest in history. We could tell right away this wasn't a cookie-cutter tour he'd delivered a hundred times. He anticipated what we wanted but paid close attention and was flexible along the way. My Roman Forum fiasco was a perfect example. After that happened, he adjusted the plan so we'd be comfortable (or at least, not pass out). He even took us to an "alimentari" for Powerades. "Electrolytes," he said in his Italian accent.

Besides watching out for us, Gino was able to explain things in a way that was interesting not only to us, but also to our kids. He even made the Vatican fun and had the teens giggling with the history of "The Fig Leaf Campaign" (the alternate covering and uncovering of the nude statues' "private parts" by various regimes throughout history).

At the end of the day, we realized we'd covered more ground, seen more sights, and been less stressed because of Gino. Not only did we get the insider's view we wanted, but we got a *customized* experience, one that had been carefully tailored to us as individuals...thanks to Gino's detective work.

Take Listening and Observation to a Higher Level

Let's go deeper into what we discussed in chapter 6: how listening is critical to building a relationship and uncovering the customer's ideal solution.

What Gino did for me, Teri, and our kids is exactly what an Unco-pyable salesperson does for their customers. He guided us through the exact experience we wanted. He asked questions about things we hadn't considered and, as a result, made recommendations for activities that weren't even on our radar. And our day was unforgettable.

Yes, we could have planned the day on our own and toured the city with our noses buried in guidebooks. When I'd fainted, someone would probably have notified "la polizia." (I have nightmares of that scenario!) Not only was disaster averted, but we had a great time.

The most successful salespeople are like Gino. They think like Sher-lock Holmes. They go much farther than mere active listening and observation. They deeply investigate everything before offering a solution. They ask more probing questions and learn everything they can about the customer so they can deliver the experience that solves their problem or delivers on their aspirations. The time you put in before you offer a solution shows you care about them as a person.

Sherlock Holmes didn't just listen to people. He took active listening and observation to a higher level, noticing intricate details that solved mysteries no one else was able to. Gino did that. When he asked, "Are there specific sights you want to see?" he didn't just accept our response and move on. Through his experience, he knew some common tourist attractions weren't really as great as they sounded, so he probed further. He'd ask, "Why do you want to go to that place?" He wanted to determine if there was an important reason, like, "That's where my parents met." If there was an important reason, he would put it on the schedule. If there wasn't, he would suggest one or two alternatives he felt would make a bigger impact on our day. That's how Sherlock Holmes would approach getting the best information.

When you care about doing a good job for your customer, your goal is to improve their business or life. The deeper you can dig, the better. By knowing your customers and their needs better than the competition, you can deliver the solution they're looking for—and, like for me and Teri, the one they haven't thought of.

Remember Power Wash Dude back in chapter 6? He missed a critical step—he skipped the Sherlock Holmes mode. He simply wasn't curious. He gave his sales presentation before he asked any questions. He missed the opportunity to deliver a customized solution based on what my friend Cheryl was looking for.

Cheryl could have cared less about the 3 Ps of Power Washing. Here's what she DID care about:

She wanted to make her house look better than ever, because she had friends coming to visit—friends she hadn't seen in years. Her friends had never seen her current house (she'd moved to a new house since they'd visited). She wanted to showcase her new home and make it look its best. She was especially concerned about the spots most visible from the front of the house (curb appeal, as they say!). She wanted her landscaping to be handled with extra care. When the job was done, she didn't want any traces of moss—she was worried about it being "blown onto the lawn." She wanted it to seem like there had never even *been* any moss.

Power Wash Dude (let's call him PWD) would have learned all that if he'd started with Sherlock Holmes mode. A good opening question would have been simple: "What prompted you to call yesterday?"

Cheryl would have been happy to tell him. (Ironically, PWD may have addressed some of her concerns, but by then she had literally tuned him out. And by the way, people never tune out when they're talking!)

If PWD had started with questions, he would have gathered the exact details to help her buy. When he switched to "Get the Yes" mode, he could have helped her imagine the transformation she was going to enjoy and the great impression her house would make on her friends!

Questions are the tools that reveal what is (and isn't) motivating our potential customers. Their answers put us in a position to bring them expertise and insights that would be hard—or impossible—to research on their own. It allows us to filter the information we give them so we present only what's relevant. We learn which behind-the-scenes details we should give them when we help them buy.

What's the Hidden Desire?

A lot of salespeople will tell you that effective selling means finding out the problem or pain the buyer wants solved and then helping them solve that problem or get rid of that pain. That's a limited way of looking at information-gathering, and it won't make you Uncopyable. If you want to become truly Uncopyable, you'll go deeper and listen with the intention of *finding ways to make the other person's life better.* That's something few salespeople focus on. Your customer connects your product/service/solution to their own perception of what that means. It's your job to educate them—but the first step is always to drill down to what really matters to them. Uncover information that causes them to think about things they wouldn't have otherwise.

Very early on in our discussion, Gino figured out, via the questions he posed in emails, that Teri and I *wanted to have a day in Rome that our daughters would remember fondly for the rest of their lives.* That was the experience we were after. We weren't visiting Rome to complete research on third-century AD Roman history for the defense of our PhD thesis. We weren't visiting Rome to engage in "retail therapy"— shopping at the elite stores of our choice. We weren't visiting Rome to be able to brag about the sights we'd seen to the members of our social circle. All of those were *possible* reasons we might have chosen to hire Gino as a guide. But the *real* reason we wanted to work with him— the *main* experience we were after—was sharing an unforgettable day with our daughters. Gino listened. He identified that motivation very early on, and then he focused like a laser beam on making it happen. When something came up that was a potential obstacle to us living that experience, he helped us to change course so that we *would* have our desired experience.

Bear in mind that your prospects may not quite know how to describe their desired experience themselves. They may need some help. Be ready to ask questions in the following groups:

Getting-to-Know-You Questions

These can help you build a connection, and they can also uncover important "backstory." Personal questions might include:

- *Tell me about your family.*

- *Tell me about your neighborhood.*

- *What got you interested in (something that you know is of interest to them)?*

- *I'm just curious—where do you see yourself in five years?*

Are these "icebreaker" questions? Yes. Can they uncover important information? Absolutely. *Listen carefully* to what you hear in response.

IT'S OUR JOB TO FIGURE OUT WHAT THE PROSPECT'S DESIRED EXPERIENCE (IF THEY KNEW IT WAS AVAILABLE) LOOKS, SOUNDS, AND FEELS LIKE...AND THEN HELP THEM BUY THE VERY THING THAT WILL MAKE THAT EXPERIENCE HAPPEN.

Tell-Me-about-the-Issue-at-Hand Questions

These can give you clues about the kind of *experience* the person is looking to step into.

- *What are you doing about this problem (or aspiration) now?*

- *What is working well?*

- *What could be better?*

- *What kinds of problems are you dealing with in this area?*

- *What keeps you up at night about this?*

- *What are you really trying to accomplish here?*

- *What's the outcome in your best-case scenario?*

Remember, when you're in Sherlock mode, you're not going to diagnose the situation or propose a solution. You might be itching to do that! Listen carefully for more clues about the kind of *experience* this individual is looking for.

Have-You-Thought-about-X Questions

"Have you thought about" questions go beyond the expressed/acknowledged needs of your customer. They address pains and aspirations that are unknown or hidden. They also address the solutions that the prospect doesn't know are attached to your product.

Zoresco, whom I mentioned earlier, is a consulting client. Zoresco sells truck bodies to fleets. But they don't just sell a generic product—they design customized solutions for each customer. Before Zoresco proposes a design, they visit the fleet's headquarters to learn and study how they're used. They uncover unique challenges and opportunities for that particular fleet. That includes the effect of a custom-designed truck body on the driver's experience. They even do ride-alongs with truck drivers to get a snapshot of "a day in the life." The result: Zoresco's customized truck bodies create a more comfortable experience, happier drivers, and higher productivity.

Increased productivity is an example of a dollars-and-cents benefit prospects might not think of. In Sherlock mode, you're learning about pain points and aspirations that aren't obvious so you can present the very best solution.

These days, the buying process often starts with an Internet search. The problem is people don't know what they don't know. That means they don't even know the right questions to ask! Without an expert to guide them, they miss important information or come to conclusions that are just plain wrong. It's happened to me: whenever I have a weird pain, the first place I go to is *WebMD*. My research usually leads me to the same conclusion: *I have a tumor.* (Thankfully, my official tumor count is zero.)

Once you've gained insight into the obvious outcomes your customer is looking for, use your Sherlock skills to uncover potential outcomes your prospective customer will benefit from. Examples of questions include the following:

- *Many of the people I have worked with have encountered (X challenge or obstacle). Has that been an issue for you?*

- *Some of what you're saying reminds me of a situation where a customer decided to do [Y] (briefly explain the specific story). Have you considered anything like that?*

- *A lot of my customers are now looking at [Z] as an option in this kind of situation. (Be ready to share a story that backs up your expertise and demonstrates the desired result.) Would that kind of outcome benefit you?*

Once again—don't take their response as a license to start reciting a spiel about how wonderful your product is. *Ask another question* and actively listen. These questions get your prospects to tell you what kind of experience they're looking for.

Here's an example: One of our clients sells a type of manufacturing machinery that operates under extremely high pressure. The price of the machinery is slightly higher than the competition's.

Our client added a new customer, one who'd been buying the cheaper, competitive brand. Here's why: while the customer was using the cheaper machine, it overheated. The result: an uncontrolled explosion of pressure and steam. Thankfully, nobody was injured. But it could have been disastrous.

That customer quickly switched to our client's product, even though it has a higher price, because it has a special safety system on every machine that prevents that exact scenario.

Ever since that happened, their salespeople ask prospects: "Is safety a priority on your factory floor?" Having a specific story makes your product's advantages meaningful. Rather than citing facts and statistics, tell a story your customer can relate to. You lead them to considerations they hadn't thought of. It can work to address objections—like price—before they even come up. You paint a picture of an outcome (either positive or negative) they hadn't pictured.

Ask WHY

I just watched a documentary on the singer Pink. The documentary gave a behind-the-scenes peek into one of her concert tours. On this tour, Pink (real name: Alecia) had her family in tow (I don't care how much help she had—this is one brave woman). In one scene, Pink had a typical conversation with her toddler, Jameson. No matter what she said, he responded with the same word: "Why?"[8]

Pink *(telling her son to leave a Band-Aid on)*: Try to leave it and don't pull it off because it needs to heal.

Jameson: Why?

Pink: That's your body's way of healing itself.

Jameson: Why?

Pink: Because you're a strong boy. And the body is a miracle and resilient.

Jameson: Why?

Pink: Can you say *resilient*?

Jameson: No.

If you've ever been around a toddler, you recognize that pattern. It can be comical—and a little frustrating. As a salesperson, "why" is a simple yet powerful word. Now, I don't recommend you ask, "Why?" over and over like a toddler would. But the right use of the word "why" will get your prospect to open up in a way they might not otherwise.

Get Comfortable with Silence

In a conversation, silence can be uncomfortable. I get it—it's tough to let the conversation lapse. Silence is an invitation to talk that's almost irresistible. Notice I say "almost." When you're in Sherlock mode, be the one who resists! Have the restraint to let the prospect/customer fill the silence. You'll uncover sales gold.

Sherlock BONUS TIP: Ask Your Customers Why They Buy

It might seem a little weird to ask your customer that question. You're the salesperson, and you should know the answer, right?

Not always. Hearing your customer explain their reasons for buying—in their own words—can be invaluable. Sometimes you come up with the answers you expect. Other times they reveal reasons that aren't obvious. Those reasons can help you sell other prospects.

Here's an example: When I worked for Walker, my customers were automotive distributors. *Their* customers were the muffler shops who installed the mufflers on their customers' cars.

I knew that if I could convert new muffler shops to Walker, my distributors would make more sales. We'd both win. I made a list of muffler shops who were using the competition's brand and started making calls. At first, my efforts failed. I ran into the same objection: PRICE.

The challenge was that both Walker's and the competitor's muffler came with a lifetime warranty. When the end customer—the person

ASKING THE RIGHT QUESTIONS, RATHER THAN RUSHING TO OFFER A SOLUTION THAT MAY NOT BE A GOOD FIT, WILL SET YOU APART FROM OTHER SALESPEOPLE.

driving the car—had a muffler installed, they got a certificate. If the muffler failed, the customer could present the certificate and get a free replacement muffler.

Walker's mufflers were better quality. I knew that. But they were more expensive. Since both brands came with a lifetime warranty, why would a muffler shop pay more for Walker products?

The answer came from one of my distributor's customers—a muffler shop who was loyal to Walker:

"We used to buy the cheaper mufflers," he told me. "It was a mistake. It cost us customers, hurt our reputation, and cut into our profits." When I asked him to explain, he said, "The cost of the muffler is minor compared to the labor cost it takes to install it. If a customer has a muffler installed and it fails, they come in for a replacement. Because of the 'lifetime warranty,' they expect it to be free. The muffler may be free, but not the labor it takes to tear the old one out and install the new one."

He shook his head. "The customer is pretty ticked when they get a bill that's almost as much as they paid when the muffler was originally installed. Sometimes we 'eat' part of the cost, which cuts into our profit. Other times we charge the customer the labor. Either way, it's not good."

Learning that was an eye-opener!

The higher-quality muffler made a huge difference because it lasted a lot longer. The less often the "lifetime warranty" had to be honored, the better for the muffler shop.

That was an "aha" moment for me. It gave me the information I needed to explain the value of our product versus the competition's— even though they both had lifetime warranties. It helped me add new muffler shop customers, boosting my distributors' sales—and mine.

Whether it's with your prospective customers or your current customers, *dig, dig, dig, and keep digging*. It's what great detectives do. It's what great salespeople do, too. Use your best Sherlock skills, and you'll be in a position to deliver a solution that's unique and Uncopyable. You'll set yourself apart from your competition, and you'll make more sales.

BONUS CONTENT AND WORKBOOK AVAILABLE AT

UNCOPYABLESALES.COM/RESOURCES

CHAPTER 8

YOUR FORTUNE IS IN THE FOLLOW-UP

Have you heard statistics like these?

> *Eighty percent of sales require five follow-up calls after the meeting.*
> *Forty-four percent of sales reps give up after one follow-up.*

I'm sure you have. I've read or heard versions of these many times.

Here's the problem. I've searched all over the Internet and can't find proof these numbers are real. Then again, do these statistics have a ring of truth to them? I'd say yes—because we've all worked with salespeople who don't follow up. We all know most sales require multiple interactions. So let's just go with these generally agreed-upon assumptions: Most sales are made through multiple contacts. And when it comes to follow-up, most salespeople suck.

We've all heard the saying, "The fortune is in the follow-up." One successful salesperson I know calls it "friendly persistence." I love that.

She credits consistent and personable follow-up in busting through her sales goals. Notice she says "friendly." As she told me, "You're not following up to give them the hard sell. You do it to stay on their mind and at the same time let them know they're on YOUR mind." While your competition is missing this crucial step in the sales process, you can use follow-up to your advantage. Make it one of your own Uncopyable secrets to win at sales.

The other day I went to the mailbox and found a handwritten note addressed to Steve and me from our Pilates teacher, Crystal. We're both her loyal Pilates students. (In case you've wondered how we stay in such peak physical condition, now you know!) Not only is Crystal our Pilates instructor, but as I've mentioned before, we also buy health products through the organization she represents. "I appreciate you guys so much," her note said. "Thanks for your support and friendship."

What a nice surprise to receive that! The simple thank-you note probably didn't take much time, but the fact that she thought of us and took the time to write us a note meant a lot. Crystal uses follow-up to make us feel like she cares about us as people, not just customers. That's just one of the reasons follow-up is an Uncopyable sales secret.

Follow-up helps you make new sales and increases repeat sales. It's an opportunity to do several things:

1. Stay Top of Mind

"Out of sight, out of mind," as the saying goes. Your prospects and customers are busy—like you, they have a lot going on. Staying on their mind is key. Even if someone contacts you because they're interested in your product or service, you need them to think of you when the time is right. Be proactive with your follow-up. And don't forget—if someone is your Moose, they're probably someone else's Moose, too. You don't want to neglect a prospect or customer and open the door for someone else to be the one they think of for your solution.

2. Advance the Sale

Just because someone doesn't buy right away doesn't mean they won't buy later. When someone says, "I'll think about it," it usually means they have questions or doubts. (I've also had prospects who were just plain sneaky—they admitted they were testing me to see if I'd actually follow up!) A customer who "needs to think about it" often doesn't have enough information or the timing isn't right. Follow-ups are the way to deliver the information they need to buy. Just as important, it's also your ongoing opportunity to learn more about what matters to them, giving you intel on how to match their needs and wants to your solution or transformation. Don't overlook your current customers, either. They're often your best prospects. Whether you're dealing with prospects or ongoing customers, you want to be aware of any changes in their situations or needs. Stay in touch so you can stay on top of new opportunities.

3. Solidify the Relationship

People buy from those they know, like, trust, and remember. In other words, people buy from people they have a relationship with. And relationships take time. Follow-up gives you a chance to build trust and enhance your connection. Focus on your prospects and customers—not only professionally, but personally. Your follow-up shows you care about them and that they're important to you. Every touchpoint is a chance to grow your relationship. When you can, use your follow-up communications to learn about THEM. The need to listen doesn't stop after the first call—or even the first sale. In relationship selling, you're constantly advancing and solidifying the sales relationship even after they buy.

The best way to be good at follow-up is to have a plan. Making a plan ahead of time makes follow-up a no-brainer. Before your first call, you researched your prospect, right? What more did you learn during your initial encounter? Use additional information you learned from your sales contact. Then, ask yourself, "Does the prospect still fit the profile of my Moose? And do they acknowledge a need? (Are they hungry?)" Reassess the customer's potential. This is important, because the size of your Moose—and their probable impact on your sales—will determine your follow-up budget in time and money. You might find out they're not your Moose after all—or no longer are. That's critical, because you don't want to waste your time on a prospect who has little or no potential.

Be sure to create variety in what you plan to send. For example, you might plan to send a thank-you note, video email, phone call, then a case study or testimonial. You can always adjust along the way, but having a plan from the start makes the steps automatic —which means you're more likely to take action.

But You Need to Stay Organized!

One of the reasons salespeople don't follow up is plain old disorganization. You can have the best intentions, great ideas, and a perfect follow-up plan. But to stay on top of it, you need to be organized. Thanks to technology, that's not hard to do. Things have come a long way since I started in sales. In the old days, I used a Day-Timer for appointments and 3" x 5" index cards to keep track of account details when I made calls. At the end of the day, I'd transfer the information into a customer folder. It wasn't super efficient, and I lived in fear of losing my Day-Timer (thankfully, that never happened).

Technology to the rescue! We now have lots of tools to use—but they work only if you use them. At least we can't lose our calendars, since all our information is "backed up on the clouds," as my dad would say.

You Need a CRM

If you work for a company with a customer relationship manager, or CRM, it's the obvious tool that will help you keep track of follow-ups. If you don't have one that's provided, you can subscribe to one on your own. Your CRM helps you keep track of customer details and what your next steps are.

The key is you have to USE your CRM consistently to stay organized. It can be easy to move on to the next task, get distracted, and forget to make notes. Include details—both business and personal—that came up during each conversation. These are critical for using later. Be sure to set reminders so nothing slips through the cracks.

What if you don't have a CRM? If you're an entrepreneur or work for an organization that doesn't have a CRM, technology can still come to your rescue. When you make your follow-up plan, enter your follow-ups into your online calendar. And be sure to set reminders! For client details, you can take advantage of a digital note-taking tool.

Tools for Follow-Up

Whenever I send a follow-up, I like to ask myself one simple question: "How would I feel if I got this?" It's tempting to stay in full-on sales mode when you follow up. But your customers want to feel the way I feel about doing business with Crystal—I'm not just a customer; I'm a friend and valued client!

Follow-up is an important part of the sales process. Good follow-up goes beyond "I'm checking in to see if you've made a decision yet." Uncopyable follow-up is engaging with prospects and future team members in uncommon, creative ways!

Don't ask for the order in every communication. If your goal is an Uncopyable sales relationship...to show you really care about your prospects and customers...make sure you balance sales-related follow-up with relationship follow-up. And the more creative you are, the better.

You should use multiple tools when following up, too. We're all familiar with the common, overused follow-up tools: email, phone calls, email, texting, messaging, and did I say email?

I get it. Of course, we want to use email! It's so easy to type something quickly and click "send." It's so easy to create one email and BLAST it out to hundreds, even thousands, of people who we know

YOUR FORTUNE IS IN THE FOLLOW-UP

just can't wait to get our sales pitch. We click that button, lean back, and congratulate ourselves for executing our powerful sales campaign! Yes, there's a place for email in our communications, but let's recognize its limitations and the fact that every one of our competitors overuses it, too.

We want to be Uncopyable, right? We want our future customers and team members to choose US. We want them to know us, like us, trust us, and remember us! And to do that, we have to behave differently. Let's look at some tools I use and recommend to set you apart.

Video Email

Of course, regular, old, impersonal email is the default communication tool these days. It's easy, free and...boring. But your goal is to stand out, right? Why not enhance your email follow-ups, like Rob Lanouette? I met Rob when I spoke for an association of senior living communities. Rob is in charge of sales for a senior living community called Wesley. One of Rob's responsibilities is sales, and he realized he had a problem: he didn't stand out. Before deciding on a senior living community, prospective residents usually research and tour multiple facilities with their family members. It makes sense that they want to compare facilities before they make a decision. This created a challenge: Rob realized that if a prospective resident visited more than a couple facilities, they literally couldn't remember which was which and who was who.

The answer: He started sending follow-up emails that included a personal video. "It's made a huge difference," he said. It's helped his sales—in fact, he credits his unique follow-up in selling out a new building they opened in record time!

With messages containing embedded videos, Rob can make face-to-face contact via email and connect in a way that's extremely personal compared to a typed email. To demonstrate, Rob sent me a sales email. WOW. It definitely made an impression. I opened the email, and there was Rob. With a big smile, he looked right at me and said, "Hello, my friend! I want you to see for yourself how I'm connecting with my prospective residents in a whole new way!" What a difference between a typed email and one with a face, eye contact, a smile, and a personal message delivered in Rob's voice. His warmth and enthusiasm came through in a way that wouldn't with typed words. I could immediately see why this method of communication gives him an Uncopyable advantage.

Handwritten Thank-You Notes

If your prospect takes the time to meet with you, send a thank-you note. At a minimum, I always send a thank-you email. But a handwritten note, or personalized video email, is much better. I just sent a thank-you note to a new client, who'd met with me on a video call. I had her address and sent her one of the "Adventure Orange" cards we have here in the office. It's always great to mention something specific about the meeting in your note. In this case, I mentioned a personal compliment she'd given me during our call. She told me she'd really enjoyed our conversation and appreciated the fact that I was "warm and approachable." I was touched and told her it really made my day—which it did! (It was also a great reminder that it never hurts to pass along the kind words that pop into our heads—they really do make a difference.)

Greeting Cards

Sending a greeting card is one of my top *Get in the Door* strategies. It's also a great way to build a sales relationship—before or after the sale. The more personal you can make it, the better.

Remember birthday cards? For the most part, they've been replaced by social media greetings (yawn), texts, and sometimes a phone call. Getting a birthday card in the mail has become a rarity (at least for me)! If you can find someone's birthday and you send an actual card, you'll stand out. Go one better and personalize your card with a picture. Some online card companies even offer gifts you can send along with the card!

Photos

It's hard to beat a photo as a follow-up. In my office, I have a framed photo I received as a follow-up to a meeting several years ago. I got it after a business dinner meeting. During the meal, the waiter had snapped a few pictures of the group. Everybody has phones with cameras these days, and we hardly noticed our pictures being taken. We all probably have more pictures taken in a week than our grandparents did in their lifetime!

Where do all these pictures go? They stay on our phones, are posted on social media, or are sometimes texted or emailed to a friend. If you want to stand out, have a picture printed and send it to them. Every drugstore can print, frame, or make gifts out of any picture. You can even have it made into a card (some drugstores do that, too).

The next time you're with a prospect or a customer, take a photo. Then, have it framed and send or deliver it to them. We've done that for years. We're amazed at how often those photos end up on someone's wall, bookshelf, or table!

(Tip: Are you meeting virtually? You can do the same with a screenshot!)

Case Studies and Testimonials

Case studies might sound intimidating, but they don't have to be. A case study is basically an example of how a specific customer successfully solved a problem or achieved an aspiration by taking the action you recommended. A simple formula for a case study is:

- Problem

- Action

- Result

Think of a customer who had a problem that was solved or an aspiration that was realized by your product or service. Why not put together your own simple case study and send it to prospects who are in a similar situation? You can easily spice up—and personalize—a case study using an online design platform.

Customer testimonials are also extremely effective. It's more persuasive to hear how great you are from a customer than to hear it from you. Think about how many e-commerce sites provide customer reviews for every product they sell, effectively changing the way people buy. Almost every time I purchase something online, I get an email: "Kay K Miller, will you rate your transaction?"

There are customers out there who spend a lot of time doing product reviews. Some even include pictures and videos. These days, we're all accustomed to using reviews to make buying decisions. Create your own version with case studies and testimonials and share them as part of your follow-up.

The most powerful type of testimonial is a video. The next time you talk to a customer who tells you how happy they are, pull out your phone and record their comments (of course, ask their permission first!). You can also schedule a quick video interview with them and ask them a few questions to get them talking. Technology makes it easy to have the audio transcribed. Not only do you end up with a video testimonial, with a few edits you have a written testimonial, too! Recording your own customer testimonials is the easiest way to proactively build your own library of social proof. And social proof is a great follow-up tool!

Books

A few years ago, Steve and I drove up the Oregon coast, stopping at the Bandon Dunes Golf Course. It's one of Steve's favorite places to play, and it's also world-famous. He was excited because he and Kelly were planning a trip there for a dad-and-daughter getaway. While we were there, we saw a book in the pro shop on the history of Bandon Dunes. We knew one of our clients is an avid golfer, and Bandon Dunes is on his bucket list. No, we didn't send him to Bandon Dunes—but we did send that book. He loved it!

Any kind of book you enjoy, or find valuable, works well. If you read an interesting book that you think a prospect or customer will appreciate, send it, along with a note.* This strategy helps

* Pssst! Here's a super-secret Uncopyable tip: It's often very easy to get an author to autograph books, especially if you buy in bulk. If you find a book you'd like to share with, say, 12 prospects and team members, search the author online. It's very common for them to have contact information. Offer to buy the books straight from the author and request he/she autograph them. If it isn't too many, sometimes they'll even personalize an inscription to your prospect. Think of the impression THAT would make!

the customer see you as a valuable resource and proves you're thinking about *them.* You can do this quickly by ordering it online and choosing to send it as a gift, allowing you to include your own message. Or buy multiple copies and send them to multiple prospects.

Business Article or Other Helpful Content

One successful salesperson I know is a voracious reader of *The Wall Street Journal.* Whenever he reads an interesting story, he thinks, *Who do I know who would find this interesting?* It allows him to send an email link with the headline, "This made me think of you," or "I thought you'd find this interesting." Share information that's interesting or useful to them, not something that relates only to what you're selling.

You can also create your own content to mail or email to your customers and prospects. I recommend something we call "Flip the FAQs." What does that mean? Basically, it's a list of questions someone should ask before buying X (your product or solution). You create the list, and you include questions *you'd like your prospective customers to ask.* These are the questions that showcase your difference. Along with the questions, the answers you provide point to YOU as the ideal solution.

Be a Connector

Whenever the opportunity arises, I try to be a resource by connecting customers who can help each other. (Obviously, I do that only if they're in completely different industries.) Being a connector can grow your customer's network—and yours. It doesn't cost anything and adds to the value you provide for everyone involved. Create one-to-one

THINK OF FOLLOW-UP SIMPLY AS REGULAR ENGAGEMENT WITH YOUR MOOSE, WHETHER THEY HAVE PURCHASED FROM YOU OR NOT.

connections when you can. The beauty of being a connector is it's very easy to manage. The best part is everybody sees it as extremely valuable! Keep your radar up for opportunities to connect your customers (in noncompeting roles, of course).

Shock and Awe

This one's a showstopper, which is why I'm repeating it. This is one of my favorite *Get in the Door* strategies, but it's also great for follow-up. When we want to make a really big impression on somebody, we put together a "shock and awe" package. The package might have *everything* I listed in chapter 5. It's packaged nicely, with each cool gift wrapped in orange tissue paper. If we know our Moose has three kids, we'll send four pairs of orange sunglasses. People absolutely flip out when they get a package.

One of our clients, Charnecke Tents, manufactures large tents—the kind used for outdoor meetings and events. Their Moose are rental companies. When Jenny, the owner, gets an order for a tent, she sends a "shock and awe" box as a thank-you! In Jenny's case, every new customer is a prospect for the other company her family owns, CCC Washers. Their companies are in Wisconsin, and Jenny builds her "shock and awe" boxes with a Wisconsin theme. She loads each one of them up with a grab bag of locally made items: candles, soap, tea, jelly, and more. She wraps each item in green tissue paper and mails them in a green box. Her customers love them (one of them called her recently to say he used every single thing in the box)! Customers not only feel appreciated, but the "shock and awe" box keeps Charnecke tents on their mind when they're ready to think about buying a tent washer.

BONUS CONTENT AND WORKBOOK AVAILABLE AT

UNCOPYABLESALES.COM/RESOURCES

CHAPTER 9

GETTING THE YES

"I just bought two Rad ebikes!" Sue, a friend of mine, emailed me with the news. Sue recently retired, and she and her husband had been interested in power bikes. "I contacted Rad to ask some questions," she said. "I didn't plan on buying, but by the end of the phone call I was so excited, I ordered two of them on the spot!"

Before she contacted Rad, Sue did a lot of research on her own. She talked to ebike owners she met, watched YouTube videos, and read reviews. By the time she talked to a Rad salesperson, she was leaning toward a Rad bike and had even chosen a specific model.

But…she ended up buying a *different model* than the one she had in mind. And she credits the salesperson, Jen, with saving her from making a mistake!

For Sue, Jen acted like our Italian guide Gino. Jen asked lots of questions and found out what was important to Sue. During their conversation, Jen brought up multiple things Sue hadn't considered. In the end, Sue said, "I'm so glad I had Jen to walk me through everything. The bikes we ended up with are perfect!"

Throughout their call, Jen was in Sherlock mode. She started with the question, "How did you hear about us?" That got Sue talking. As Sue talked, Jen asked more questions about everything from fitness and activity level to interests, lifestyle, and more. "Do you want to ride on the road or on trails? Is convenience important? Comfort? Maneuverability?" As Sue answered, Jen probed and asked even more questions.

Jen continued to listen during the conversation and made sure she understood what she was hearing from Sue. She used Sue's own words to confirm they were on the same page. She summarized what she'd learned: they were retired, owned an RV, and were active enough for short bike rides but wanted the flexibility of the power assist to take longer rides. They wanted to ride on the street but also do some light off-road riding.

"It was really fun," Sue said afterward. "Jen really created a visual, taking me through a bunch of different scenarios we could use these bikes for, like making quick runs to the store when we're camping. By accessorizing with baskets, we can skip the hassle of driving the RV for short trips." Jen helped Sue imagine the freedom, flexibility, and sense of adventure these bikes would bring to their lives. As Sue put it, "It turned out to be about a whole lot more than a pair of bikes."

Jen educated Sue on some specific benefits that surprised her. Sue had figured they'd need a bike rack and was excited when Jen told her they could skip the expense and hassle by choosing a fold-up bike. "We won't need to worry about locking them up when we leave. The bikes are so compact, we can store them in the RV. Talk about convenient!"

Since Jen learned it was important for them to have something that wouldn't be too bulky, she talked about the advantages of having a mini ebike. "Before I talked to Jen, I didn't like the idea of the smaller wheels.

But she explained how they're engineered. For our needs, the wheel size won't matter. And they'll be a lot easier to transport and handle."

By the end of the call, Sue told me, her casual interest had grown into a feeling of "I want these NOW!" She went with Jen's final recommendation: the RadMini Step-Thru 2, which would fit everything Sue and her husband needed and be not only the safest to ride and handle, but also the easiest to get on and off. "This is the bike I think you'll be happiest with. I think you'll really love them!" Jen said. She recommended some bike accessories, creating a customized version just for them.

"I'll take TWO!" Sue said and grabbed her credit card. "I couldn't have been happier with the process," Sue said. At the end of the call, Jen gave Sue her cell phone number in case she had any questions.

When I got Sue's email, I had to hear the story in person. As I listened to Sue describe the "delightful conversation," as she put it, I was impressed by the way the selling/buying process happened so seamlessly. It was a back-and-forth interaction between an interested customer and a great salesperson. Jen clearly believed in her product and cared about the customer. The conversation had nothing to do with a "sales pitch." Sue was part of the process on every level. She felt heard and understood, and she believed that Jen's recommendation truly helped her make the right decision—one she wouldn't have been able to make on her own. It was a definite win-win!

Do you see the commonalities between my approach with Jerry Cornell, Gino's approach with Teri and me, and Jen's approach with Sue?

As salespeople, all of us worked hard in the beginning to develop a mutually trusting relationship. Once we got in the door, we didn't immediately pitch hard. We took it slow and learned as much as we could about our prospects' needs, desires, and frustrations. We all approached our information-gathering like Sherlock Holmes. We practiced active listening and observation, probing deeper into our customer's seen and unseen needs. These relationship-centric efforts further solidified the mutually trusting relationship we had worked hard to establish.

Don't Sweat "Closing"

Remember when I wrote in the first chapter about *The Wall Street Journal* article saying young people are turned off by sales careers? They still think of selling the "old school" way: cold calls, manipulation, and high-pressure closing techniques.

I've never approached the sales relationship that way. I've never looked at prospects and customers as adversaries.

Boiled down, the Uncopyable sales process is based on mutually agreed-to next steps.

1. The prospect has to agree to meet with you (or connect in some other way).

Nothing happens until the first step happens, right? You need to get in the door!

TO BE UNCOPYABLE, DO WHAT IT TAKES TO UNDERSTAND THE CUSTOMER, PRIORITIZE THE RELATIONSHIP OVER THE SALE, AND COMMIT TO A WIN-WIN OUTCOME.

2. The prospect has to agree with your analysis of their situation, needs, and desires.

Sue's buying process started with her own research. On their phone call, Jen's first job was to learn and understand where Sue was coming from. What did she know about Rad Bikes? What was her perception? Jen went into Sherlock mode and learned everything she could about Sue and her husband. As in the story of Gino, Jen asked the right questions and uncovered Sue's wants, likes, and priorities. By digging, Jen uncovered what really mattered to Sue and addressed possible objections that might come up.

3. The prospect has to believe you have their best interests at heart.

Regardless of whether you have a long getting-to-know-you period or one phone call, like Jen had with Sue, you are looking to build trust. Throughout the call, Jen repeated what Sue said, using Sue's own words. Jen used phrases like, "It sounds like..." to make sure she understood Sue's needs, concerns, and desires.

Jen painted a clear picture of the experience Sue wanted. She also helped her realize what she *didn't* want. One example was the need for a bike rack. Sue figured it was a necessity. Yes, it would be a hassle, but she'd just have to deal with it. But when Jen described the actual process of having to unload and load the bikes every time, Sue realized what a pain in the butt it would be. Jen helped her imagine a much more pleasant scenario—simply folding the bikes and popping them into the RV.

This process helped Sue clarify some of her thoughts—and even gave her a few "aha" moments. And it helped Sue believe Jen truly wanted to help.

4. The prospect has to agree with your recommendation.

Jen's recommendation addressed all the issues Sue had considered—and some she hadn't. Jen guided her toward making a buying decision she was super jazzed about. By listening and understanding Sue's situation and caring about Sue's experience, Jen became a trusted advisor in a short period of time.

As I said, by the end of the call, Sue wanted two bikes ASAP! Jen didn't even have to ask for the order.

When you've reached step four, you aren't using old tricks, hard closing techniques, or manipulation. Essentially, you're done, and it's just a matter of getting a "yes" on the next mutually agreed-to step. After I've delivered a presentation or proposal, I usually go with something casual, along the lines of "Does that sound good to you?" or even just "Sound good?"

The beauty of the Rad ebike example is it shows that all of the sales steps can happen in a single phone call! In many sales situations, getting the customer to BUY happens over a longer period of time. You may need to go through multiple next steps, gradually moving them closer to the sale.

When I met Jerry Cornell of Cornell Auto Parts, he swore he'd never do business with Walker again. I was able to win back his business (a great feeling!). He eventually ended up stocking our full product line in the warehouse.

But that didn't happen overnight.

Between the time I first met Jerry and the time he placed his full restocking order, I took him through a series of "next steps." He gradually came to see me as a trusted advisor.

Next Step marketing is something we recommend. But the Next Step philosophy applies equally to sales.

That first time, when Jerry vented his frustration, the recommendation I made was simply to allow me to make another sales call. Between the two calls, I took small actions to build trust. On my initial call, I told him I would send him a catalog on a new product, and I did. Then, I sent him a thank-you note. Whenever I told him I'd follow up, I made sure I called when I said I would.

My next step was to recommend a small assortment of performance products, ones his current supplier didn't carry. He agreed to a very limited stock. At that point, I continued to build trust—and the relationship. Whenever I went to Port Angeles, I'd take him to lunch. I took the time to get to know him better.

Gradually, he brought in more products, until he'd added the full line. Meanwhile, I watched his account like a hawk. I tracked his orders and kept in touch with him. I gave him great...make that *Uncopyable...* customer service.

Jerry and I built a solid relationship. He eventually bought—and sold—a lot of Walker products.

Each time he bought more, I went through the steps it took to understand, summarize, and present his desired outcome; make my recommendation; and get mutual agreement. Those are the steps Gino went through for Teri and me. And that's what Jen did on the phone with Sue.

Your Next Step

Of course, the actual process isn't always the same. Every situation is unique. You may be selling Rad ebikes, a health product, or multi-million-dollar rotary transfer machines. The steps might be managed differently, but the goal is always the same—to understand the customer and deliver an outcome that's meaningful to *them*. That includes an outcome they might not have even known about!

Your ultimate goal as a salesperson is to become a trusted advisor. Jen was able to establish herself as a trusted advisor on a single phone call. Jerry didn't trust me until I proved myself—and that took time. When your customer trusts you and they know you have their best interests at heart, they'll respect your recommendation. As Sue put it, "Jen saved me from making a mistake!"

Remember the customer who said, "We buy Leslie"? Your customers buy you. You represent the special sauce—that thing they can't get anywhere else.

To be an Uncopyable salesperson, do what it takes to truly understand the customer. Take the time to develop trust. Be committed to delivering the outcome that gets the customer excited.

Finally, don't just tell them you care. Prove it.

That's what it takes to be Uncopyable.

BONUS CONTENT AND WORKBOOK AVAILABLE AT

UNCOPYABLESALES.COM/RESOURCES

TRUST ME, THIS TAKES DETERMINATION

NOOOO!!!!

Steve and I were at The Home Course in DuPont, Washington, watching our daughter, Kelly, play golf in a high school tournament. Tournaments like this one were important, because she was working toward something big: her goal was to earn a scholarship to play D1 college golf.

As usual, we followed Kelly, watching from a distance. All was well until the fourth hole—a par three. Her tee shot sailed high, then landed in a deep sand trap next to the green.

Ugh. This wasn't an ordinary sand trap. This sand trap was bordered by a vertical wall of railroad ties—an obstacle created by some evil golf course designer to make the hole extra challenging.

Kelly's ball sat snug against a railroad tie. She had no shot.

I'll spare you the gory details, but it took her a total of seven—yes, SEVEN—shots to get out of the trap. This was a par three, which meant it should have taken her only three shots to get her ball from the tee into the hole. On that hole, she ended up getting a huge, horrible, and embarrassing score of TEN.

I'm sure the stress of watching shaved several years off my life. I'll never forget that day. But here's what stuck with me the most: she never gave up.

Kelly still had 14 long and lonely holes to play. That day, Kelly shot a total score of 80. Par for The Home Course is 72. Here's what that means: besides the fourth hole, *Kelly played the other fourteen holes even par.* Before and after her disastrous fourth hole, she played a great round. And that's the kind of grit D1 college coaches look for.

"Did you hear about the girl that got a 10 on number four and shot even par for the other 17 holes?" I could hear the buzz afterward—it was the talk of the day. Everybody heard about it—including the college coaches who were recruiting their future college teams.

How did she keep it together when things went so horribly wrong?

"My goal was to play D1 college golf," she said. "I was determined to achieve it."

"After all those swings, it was hard to keep it together," she admitted. "I had to fight back the tears. I was so humiliated, but I wasn't going to give up." Swing after swing, she kept her cool. It took sheer willpower for her to keep her head in the game, but that grit is exactly what top coaches look for.

Two years later, she accepted a spot on the D1 Portland State University golf team on scholarship. She played and lettered all four years, was on the division championship team, and set a school record for the highest finish in the NCAA tournament.

Just like overcoming a fear of failure, your determination to succeed has to do with your mindset. Determination is what it takes to convince

DETERMINATION MAKES THE DIFFERENCE BETWEEN FAILURE AND SUCCESS.

yourself to make an extra sales call, learn more about a potential customer, or spend additional time planning an important presentation. That determination means the difference between failure and success.

Angela Duckworth, author of the book *Grit*, said this in an April 2021 TED Talk:

> *Grit is passion and perseverance for very long-term goals. Grit is having stamina. Grit is sticking with your future, day in, day out, not just for the week, not just for the month, but for years—and working really hard to make that future a reality.*[9]

A determined mindset is something you choose. It's a decision that's under your control. Anyone can make the decision to be determined; to not back down, not give up. Anyone can make the decision, but not everyone does.

As we come to the end of *Uncopyable Sales Secrets*, I want to leave you with this:

That's just the way it is. But Uncopyable salespeople have grit. They stick with it, weathering the bad times and thriving in the good times, because they recognize that their sales success is directly proportional to their commitment to their greater "why."

Decide to become an Uncopyable salesperson. Build your sense of determination by focusing on the outcome you want, and be committed to it. Consider the three levels of your "why":

1. How your success will affect you personally

2. How your success will affect others in your circle (prospects, customers, team members, friends, family members)

3.   How your success will impact the world

How will your determination to succeed affect you on a personal level? Just like we admire others who overcome challenges, we feel good about ourselves when we do the same. When we give our best, especially in the face of adversity, it makes us proud of who we are. Appreciate the mental strength and confidence you will gain from committing to your sales success.

Consider, too, how your success will affect your income, your lifestyle, the house you live in, the dream vacation you want, your ability to send your kids to college, and your ability to donate to your favorite cause.

Then, think about the effect of your success on others. What will it mean to your customers? When you think of sales as helping your customers get what they want, you'll make a positive impact on their businesses and lives.

Think about what your success will mean to your family and others you care about. I want my family to be proud of me, and I want my success to expand the horizon of what's possible for them.

What will your success mean to the world? How will it enable you to serve others you don't know? How will it create a ripple effect, helping others help themselves? How will it give you the financial means to give back to your community and society as a whole?

Once you determine your "why," use it to drive your sales success. Don't just bend or break the rules—change the game entirely. Serve your Moose by fostering meaningful relationships that result in a win-win for both you and your customer.

Remember, there's no one just like you. What you offer to your customers is different than anyone else. What you sell is a package.

The package obviously includes that thing you're selling, but the most important part of the package is YOU. You are unique. What you bring to the table is your ultimate Uncopyable sales secret.

Don't make this overwhelming; small changes add up! Pick one or two things from this book to work on first. Once you master one or two, add something else. Stick with it, and you'll experience more and more sales success, until one day you'll look back and realize you truly have become an Uncopyable salesperson.

Expand your Uncopyable sales toolkit with bonus content available at
UNCOPYABLESALES.COM/RESOURCES

NOTES

1. Patrick Thomas, "The Pay Is High and Jobs Are Plentiful, but Few Want to Go Into Sales," *The Wall Street Journal*, July 14, 2021, https://www.wsj.com/articles/the-pay-is-high-and-jobs-are-plentiful-but-few-want-to-go-into-sales-11626255001.

2. Kendra Cherry, "How Experience Changes Brain Plasticity," *VeryWellMind.com*, last updated February 3, 2021, https://www.verywellmind.com/what-is-brain-plasticity-2794886.

3. Ibid.

4. Diana Coker, "73 Creative Job Titles in Corporate America," *The HR Digest*, February 8, 2020, https://www.thehrdigest.com/73-creative-job-titles-in-corporate-america/.

5. "Opportunity Cost," *New Oxford American Dictionary*, 3rd ed., ed. Angus Stevenson and Christina A. Lindberg (Oxford, UK: Oxford University Press, 2010), Oxford Reference, accessed November 28, 2021, https://www.oxfordreference.com/view/10.1093/acref/9780195392883.001.0001/m_en_us1273667.

6. Peter Drucker, *The Practice of Management* (New York: HarperCollins, 1954), 37.

7. Dale Carnegie, *How to Win Friends and Influence People* (New York: Gallery Books, 1936), 81.

8. *Pink: All I Know So Far*, directed by Michael Gracey (2021; Culver City, CA: Amazon Studios, 2021), Amazon Prime.

9. Angela Lee Duckworth, "Grit: The Power of Passion and Perseverance," *TED.com*, April 2021, https://www.youtube.com/watch?v=H14bBuluwB8&utm_campaign=Youtube+CutDowns+&utm_medium=bitly&utm_source=Description.

ACKNOWLEDGMENTS

I'm extremely grateful for all the help and support I had in writing this book!

To Jennifer Janechek—my editor (and now friend), thanks for taking my book and making it better. You put your heart into every page, and my book felt like so much more than a job to you. And to the entire Sound Wisdom team—thank you for bringing this book to life!

To Steve—thanks for believing in me, cheering for me, and always being by my side. To Kelly—thank you for inspiring me with your determination, and for your ongoing encouragement.

To those of you who generously took time to share the stories in the book—thank you. And to those who shared stories that didn't make this book...I'm saving my notes for the next one!

To my friends and family who supported me along the way—thank you. And to my customers and clients, many of whom have become friends—I appreciate each one of you.

ABOUT THE AUTHOR

Kay Miller is an expert on Uncopyable Sales. As the first woman ever hired for outside sales by Amerock, a division of Anchor Hocking, she built her formidable sales career by emphasizing long-term relationships over one-time deals. Kay was later hired by Walker Exhaust, one of the largest automotive exhaust companies in the world. While there, she was named Walker's Salesperson of the Year, an accolade that earned her the nickname "Muffler Mama."

Kay has been a top sales performer ever since and now speaks and consults to help others maximize their sales success using the Uncopyable Sales philosophy.

Kay lives in the Pacific Northwest with her husband, Steve, and cat, Sam. Her favorite activities include skiing, hiking, and spending time with their adult daughter, Kelly.

CONNECT WITH KAY

 linkedin.com/in/millerkay/

kay@uncopyablesales.com

Build an UNCOPYABLE life and business

WITH THESE TITLES FROM SOUND WISDOM.

LEARN MORE AT
beuncopyable.com/resources.

UPGRADE YOUR LIBRARY WITH
DOZENS OF CLASSIC BOOKS FROM
BEST-SELLING AUTHORS LIKE...

NAPOLEON HILL

ZIG ZIGLAR

EARL NIGHTINGALE

CAVETT ROBERT

GEORGE S. CLASON

W. CLEMENT STONE

AND MANY MORE!

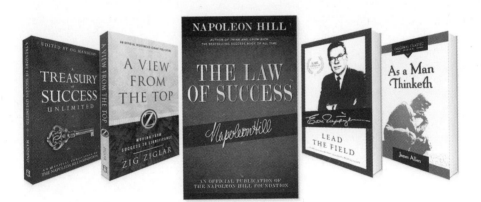

CLAIM YOUR ADDITIONAL

FREE BOOKS & RESOURCES:

WWW.SOUNDWISDOM.COM/CLASSICS